Benefit-Risk Balance
for Marketed Drugs:
Evaluating Safety Signals

Report of CIOMS Working Group IV

CI MS

Geneva 1998

ACKNOWLEDGEMENTS

The Council for International Organizations of Medical Sciences is greatly indebted to the members of CIOMS Working Group IV, on Benefit-Risk Balance for Marketed Drugs: Evaluating Safety Signals, and to the drug regulatory authorities and pharmaceutical companies they represented, for the efficient and expeditious way in which they brought this project to its successful conclusion. Special thanks are due to the co-chairs, Dr Win Castle and Dr Murray Lumpkin, for their capable leadership, to Ms Susan Roden, the secretary of the Group, and to Dr Arnold J. Gordon, editor of the full report, who very effectively coordinated, collected and edited the contributions of its individual members. We thank also Ms Salpie Leylekian, Dr Gordon's secretary, for typing and collating the many drafts of the manuscript, and Dr James Gallagher for his assistance in the editing of the final report.

TABLE OF CONTENTS

VISION

It is the hope of CIOMS Working Group IV that manufacturers and regulators will endorse and adopt the proposed systematic approach to the evaluation and reporting of the balance between benefits and risks of a marketed medicinal product with a suspected major safety problem. Strategies are recommended for improving communication between, and the sharing of action by, regulators and manufacturers, designed to strengthen decision-making in the interest of public health. We also envisage that those performing benefit-risk evaluation under these circumstances will subscribe to the following key principles and practices:

- Although evaluation and decisions are made on behalf of the at-risk population from a public-health perspective rather than that of the individual patient, the needs and perspectives of the different stake-holders and constituencies affected will be carefully taken into account.

- Although each instance of a safety issue is unique, all parties will adopt consistent practices in analysis and reporting.

- A benefit-risk evaluation should always be conducted relative to no therapy or to properly chosen comparator drugs and other treatments; to facilitate comparison between alternatives, standard graphical risk-profile representations will be routinely used.

- It will normally not be sufficient to evaluate only the effect of the new problem ("signal") on the benefit-risk relationship; a re-examination of the entire safety profile, or at least of the most prominent/important adverse drug reactions relative to other treatments, is recommended.

- Deciding the appropriate action subsequent to a benefit-risk evaluation requires "good decision-making practices"; in the assessment and decision-making processes the basis and rationale of decisions should be transparent and inter-agency cooperation should be encouraged.

The Working Group hopes also that research will be undertaken in several poorly explored or inadequately developed areas of significance to benefit-risk weighing, including metrics for weighing the relative severity/ seriousness of different adverse drug reactions; expansion of knowledge in the natural history of diseases in target populations and in the aetiology and mechanisms of drug-induced diseases; personal perception/acceptance of risks relative to benefits (how much benefit is needed to accept what level of risk); approaches to better quantification of the benefit-risk relationship; and use of formal decision theory in the decision-making process.

In summary, the CIOMS Working Group foresees a harmonized approach to the analysis, reporting and decision-making steps involved in a re-examination of benefit-risk weighing when an important new safety issue arises. It also envisages further research in this area to improve our ability to refine the results, conclusions and actions taken on behalf of patients.

Comments are invited and should be sent to Dr Zbigniew Bankowski, Secretary-General, CIOMS, c/o WHO, Avenue Appia, 1211 Geneva 27, Switzerland.

PREFACE

This is the fifth in a series of contributions from the CIOMS Working Groups on Drug Safety. This collaboration between representatives of regulatory authorities and drug manufacturers, originating in 1986, represents a commitment to improving and standardizing international reporting of adverse drug reactions and other aspects of pharmacovigilance, with a vision of better understanding and communication of matters relating to the safety of medicinal products. Although the safety or risks associated with medicines must always be judged in relation to the accompanying benefits, there are no standard, systematic approaches to the deceptively simple notion of weighing or balancing risks against benefits, especially when important new information on marketed drugs becomes available. The prior efforts of the CIOMS Working Groups have been a natural evolution towards the development of guidance in this difficult area.

CIOMS I (1990) established the now widely adopted practice of using the "CIOMS I reporting form" for standardized international reporting of individual cases of serious, unexpected adverse drug reactions. Project IA developed a set of standard data elements for individual adverse-reaction reports and their specifications for electronic reporting, which contributed to a similar initiative under the auspices of the International Conference on Harmonization (ICH). CIOMS II proposed a standard for periodic safety update reports, which has been adopted extensively since the publication of the report in 1992; it also served as a basis for the development of the official ICH guideline for such reports. CIOMS III (1995) developed proposals for international harmonization of the practical aspects of defining, creating and modifying the sections of data sheets or package inserts that contain safety information. It elaborated the concept introduced under CIOMS II of a manufacturer's Core Data Sheet for a product and the Core Safety Information (CSI) it contains.

CIOMS IV is to some extent an extension of CIOMS II and III. It examines the theoretical and practical aspects of how to determine whether a potentially major, new safety signal signifies a shift, calling for significant action, in the established relationship between benefits and risks; it also provides guidance for deciding what options for action should be considered and on the process of decision-making should such action be required. This is not a scholarly treatise on benefit-risk analysis. Rather, it suggests pragmatic approaches to reassessing the benefit-risk relationship, to producing a standard report describing the results of such an effort, and to good decision-making practices.

I. OVERVIEW

A. Background

The comparative evaluation or weighing of benefits (positive effects) and risks (potential harm) of various medical options for treatment, prophylaxis, prevention or diagnosis is essential. It is done during research and development on new medical products or procedures (such as surgery), or by a regulatory authority deliberating the approval or withdrawal of a product or some intermediate action, by a physician on behalf of a patient, or by the patient. Such weighing, whether implicit or explicit, is at the heart of decision-making in medicine and health care.

This apparently straightforward concept is expressed through such terms as *benefit to risk ratio, benefit-risk difference, benefit vs. risk, therapeutic margin, therapeutic index* and others. Regrettably, in spite of common and frequent use, none of these inexact expressions has been adequately defined or is easily quantifiable with a summary statistic. Moreover, although regulators and companies routinely make decisions driven by the balance between benefits and risks, however they are measured, there are no generally agreed procedures or regulatory guidelines for conducting and acting upon benefit-risk assessment.

Nevertheless, the European Union, for example, requires manufacturers to conduct "adequate ongoing monitoring and benefit/risk evaluation during the post-authorization period" with the aim of ensuring that "safety hazards are minimized and the benefits of treatment maximized by appropriate action."[1] Other regulatory bodies make reference to benefit-risk assessment in relation to product development and approval, to the effect of new adverse-reaction reports on a marketed product's profile (e.g., Germany), and in relation to pharmacovigilance in general. The Working Group is aware of only one detailed regulatory technical guide on benefit-risk evaluation; it deals with the special topic of carcinogenicity (*Reviewers Guide for Risk/Benefit Assessment of Drugs with Carcinogenic Potential*, Health Protection Branch, Drugs Directorate, Canada).

---

[1] *Notice to Applicants for Marketing Authorizations for Medicinal Products for Human Use in the European Community*, Chapter V, Pharmacovigilance: 5. On-Going Pharmacovigilance Evaluation During the Post-authorization Period, December 1994 (Brussels, III/5944/94) and revisions (in preparation).

Various approaches have been suggested to benefit-risk assessment during the development of new medicines[2, 3, 4, 5] but little has been published on marketed drugs, though they have much greater immediate consequences for the public health than drugs under development. An advisory panel of the Canadian Public Health Association has prepared reports[6, 7] on benefit, risk and cost management of prescription drugs, including a review of benefit-risk methodologies and risk management strategies, as well as recommendations on communication and awareness programmes for the public. Another particularly interesting presentation of ideas and views on benefit-risk decisions in licensing applications, licensing changes, and patient care, which included use of actual examples, is based on a 1985 workshop of the Centre for Medicines Research (UK).[8] Other recommended readings are found in the proceedings of two conferences dedicated to risk perception, risk management and benefit-risk assessment[9, 10] and in a treatise by the Royal Society (London) on analysis, perception and management of risk.[11]

Over the years, limitations have been imposed on the use of some marketed drugs; between 1961 and 1994, 131 products were withdrawn from various markets for reasons related to safety.[12] Although some of the relevant data are available, rarely are the process and rationale of the decisions made known. In a recent case (ketorolac and gastrointestinal or

---

[2] Spilker, B. Incorporating Benefit-to-Risk Determinations in Medicine Development, *Drug News and Perspectives*, 7 (1), February 1994, 53-59.

[3] Chuang-Stein, C.A. New Proposal for Benefit-less-risk Analysis in Clinical Trials, *Controlled Clinical Trials*, 15: 30-43, 1994.

[4] Methods and Examples for Assessing Benefit/Risk and Safety for New Drug Applications, Proceedings of a DIA Workshop, *Drug Information Journal*, 27: 1011-1049, 1993.

[5] Cocchetto, D. and Nardi, R.V. Benefit/Risk Assessment of Investigational Drugs: Current Methodology, Limitations and Alternative Approaches, *Pharmacotherapy*, 6: 286-303, 1986.

[6] *Benefit, Risk and Cost Management of Drugs.* Report of the CPHA National Advisory Panel on Risk/Benefit Management of Drugs. Canadian Public Health Association, January 1993.

[7] *Tools Employed in the Measurement of the Risks and Benefits of Drugs* — A Literature Review for the Canadian Public Health Association's National Panel on Risk/Benefit Management of Drugs. Curry Adams and Associates, Ottawa, Ontario, Canada, July 1991.

[8] Walker, S.R. and Asscher, A.W. *Medicines and Risk/Benefit Decisions*, MTP Press Limited, London, 1987.

[9] Horisberger, B. and Dinkel, R., Editors. *The Perception and Management of Drug Safety Risks.* Springer-Verlag, Berlin, 1989.

[10] Dinkel, R., Horisberger, B. and Tolo, K. W. Editors. *Improving Drug Safety — A Joint Responsibility.* Springer-Verlag, Berlin, 1991.

[11] *Risk: Analysis, Perception and Management.* Report of a Royal Society Study Group. The Royal Society, London, 1992.

[12] Spriet-Pourra, C. and Auriche, M. *Drug Withdrawal From Sale*, 2nd edition, SCRIP Reports, Richmond, UK, March 1994.

post-operative haemorrhage) the same data reviewed by different Member States of the European Union led to different benefit-risk assessments and regulatory actions.[13] Similarly, different actions were taken in regard to the association of aspirin with Reye's syndrome. In the United Kingdom, manufacturers voluntarily withdrew paediatric aspirin from the home market and added new warnings in respect of other preparations; in other countries, including the United States, warnings were added to product information but no products were withdrawn.[14]

The concept of benefit-risk weighing and its difficulties are not unique to the development and use of medicinal products; much work on this topic has been done in relation to the environment, food additives and chemicals. Useful models are also available from clinical practice, in which surgery and other modalities in addition to pharmaceuticals have been the subject of benefit-risk assessment.

It was against this background that the Working Group decided to focus its efforts in this complex subject on developing some guidance for regulators and manufacturers on assessing the balance between benefits and risks of *marketed* products with a newly established or suspected major safety problem. The balance could also be altered by the appearance of a favourable or unfavourable change in benefits to patients or by an improvement in the expected risk profile. Such a change is relatively unusual but its assessment is based on the same principles and methods.

Signals of potential safety problems with marketed medicines represent a broad spectrum of severity and impact on the public health. Most signals will not merit the type of formal benefit-risk evaluation proposed here by the Working Group, though the concepts are regarded as generally useful in any periodic or special evaluation of relative benefits and risks. The appearance of a new but relatively insignificant adverse reaction may require only a routine change in product information (data sheets, labelling, etc.). CIOMS Working Group III developed criteria and procedures for such a change, on the basis of strength of evidence and the concept of threshold for inclusion.[15]

---

[13] Summers, K. Crisis Management — Handling a Collapse in Confidence, *Scrip Magazine*, June 1995, 53-56. See also, Ketorolac PMS Study Published, *SCRIP*, No. 2103, February 16, 1996, p. 26.

[14] Paediatric Aspirin Withdrawn in UK, *SCRIP*, No. 1112, June 18, 1987, p. 5. Commission on Reye's/ Aspirin, *SCRIP*, No. 1180, February 18, 1987, p. 27. ASA/Reye's Syndrome Swedish Warning, *SCRIP*, No. 1272, January 8/13, 1988, p. 12.

[15] *Guidelines for Preparing Core Clinical-Safety Information on Drugs*, Report of CIOMS Working Group III, Council of International Organizations of Medical Sciences, Geneva, 1995.

When, then, is it necessary or appropriate to undertake the formal process developed here? The Working Group suggests that consideration be given to whether there has been a "major shift" in the balance between benefits and risks. "Major" and "shift" cannot be defined to fit all medicines and circumstances; it is always a matter of judgment to decide when the threshold for investigation and analysis has been reached. This decision may depend on the unique characteristics of the medicine and its intended use (e.g., urgency of its indications, availability of therapeutic alternatives) and on the nature of the adverse reaction and the ability to predict, detect, intervene or prevent it. In essence, the higher threshold for such a comprehensive re-evaluation than for routine or simple changes in product information is reached when a significant change is suspected to have taken place in the generally understood benefit-risk relationship. The change will usually be related to the seriousness, severity or frequency of the reaction and may be expected to result in significant changes in product information or marketing status (e.g., new contraindications, substantial restrictions on indications or treated populations, mandates for further research, or withdrawal of the product from use).

This broad topic raises many technical issues as well as complex ethical questions about the responsibility of a health authority or a company for assessing medicinal products, a process that ultimately affects an individual patient. There are no set methods that are applicable to all benefit-risk assessments; each case will be more or less different, but for all cases there are fundamental approaches and common points to consider, and this report attempts to summarize them.

Appendix A lists the members of the Working Group and summarizes its activities over the course of this project.

B. Content, Scope and Definitions

In formulating its proposals the Working Group developed, reviewed and made use of actual case histories (Appendix B) taken from the experience of companies and regulators in several countries:

- quinine and allergic haematological events (US)
- felbamate and blood dyscrasias (EU, US)
- dipyrone (metamizole) and agranulocytosis (US, Sweden)
- temafloxacin and renal impairment and hypoglycaemia in the elderly (US, EU)

- remoxipride and blood dyscrasias (Sweden)

- clozapine and agranulocytosis (Europe, US, South America)

- sparfloxacin and phototoxicity (EU, Japan, other countries)

Chapter II, sections B, C and D, uses these examples and other material to illustrate basic principles and methodologies as well as to suggest ways of displaying data, in connection with benefit estimation, risk estimation and benefit-risk evaluation. Once an analysis is completed, companies and regulators separately or jointly must consider the various options for action, between the extremes of doing nothing and immediate withdrawal of a product from the market (Chapter II, section E). Chapter III covers the decision-making process on the best options, follow-up and responsibilities; it includes a summary of the results of a small survey of regulators and companies, carried out by the Working Group, on decision-making processes and the use of outside experts.

Figure 1 provides a conceptual summary of the possible steps and processes of benefit-risk assessment. The material covered by the Working Group begins with the box labelled Signal Evaluation, in which the suspected risk is estimated (Chapter IIC), and, if the signal is confirmed, the process continues as shown in the Figure and elaborated in Chapters II and III.

There are no standard, widely acknowledged definitions of the terms *benefit* and *risk* as applied to medicine and particularly to medicinal products. These and other terms, as used in the context of this report, are defined and explained in the Glossary.

It is a frustrating aspect of benefit-risk evaluation that there is no defined and tested algorithm or summary metric that combines benefit and risk data and that might permit straightforward quantitative comparisons of different treatment options, which in turn might aid in decision-making. Rarely is it possible to express the relationship between benefits and risks quantitatively with simple units of measure (as a ratio or difference, for example), although attempts have been made, as Chapter IID indicates.

Nevertheless, no matter how the relationship between benefits and risks of a given treatment is measured or described, the measurement or description should never be an absolute one. According to the circumstances, the comparisons should apply to alternative medicinal products, non-medicinal modalities, or indeed no treatment. They may apply also to different doses or dosage forms of the same medication, whether for the same or different indications, or even to a combination of pharmaceutical and other options.

Figure 1. Overview of a Benefit-Risk Evaluation Process

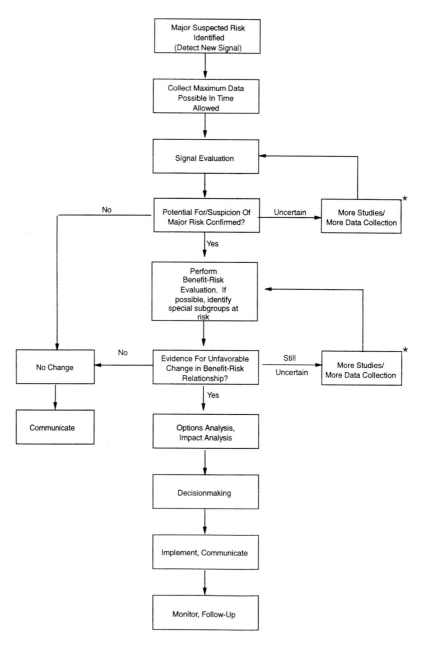

* The nature of the suspected risk and other circumstances will influence whether it is advisable or practical to delay the evaluation process. Analysis and action may be necessary in the face of varying degrees of uncertainty.

C. General Principles and Limitations

The Working Group realized there were matters that were not appropriate to the purposes of this report or possible to resolve in its context, though all were germane to the subject of benefit and risk. Chapter IV, *Unaddressed and unresolved issues*, summarizes those topics and demonstrates the breadth of issues that the Group considered. In addition, the following special points should be noted when reviewing this CIOMS IV proposal.

1. The comparative benefit-risk assessments to which this report refers relate to marketed medicinal products. Signals of adverse reactions of medical importance arise typically from market experience, usually through spontaneous reports, but may surface also in large post-marketing or other studies. However, information from all sources must be used and the same principles apply when the signal for an important safety issue surfaces in a clinical development programme in countries where the drug may not yet be on the market.

2. The public-health perspective taken here requires the collection and analysis of data from many and varied sources. One of the more difficult unresolved questions is how such an aggregate approach may be extrapolated and made relevant to a specific patient in specific circumstances. In that sense, this approach addresses the population at risk, not the patient at risk. The latter is the province of the physician (what is the best treatment for an individual under specific circumstances?).

3. A signal may indicate a possible emergency (e.g., an imminent hazard to the population at risk), which calls for crisis management measures. Although this adds to the pressure on the parties concerned, a methodical approach to a thorough benefit-risk evaluation as discussed in this report is still necessary.

4. Typically, a benefit-risk reassessment is prompted by the appearance of a particular sign, symptom, symptom-complex or diagnosis, and one automatically tends to restrict the investigation to the particular signal. However, in weighing the benefits and risks of a drug against alternatives (or no treatment) in the light of a new, important risk, the impact of the new information must be reviewed in the total context of the drug's use. Thus, it will usually be necessary to review its entire benefit-risk profile in the light of available treatment options (see Chapter IID).

5. The nature or source of the data (e.g., from clinical trials, spontaneous reports, observational studies, non-clinical experiments) will determine which of the different available methodological and analytical approaches will be used to estimate and analyse benefits and risks. This

report places more emphasis on the estimation of risks than of benefits; the reader is referred to standard texts and articles, such as those cited, for the usual details.

6. In addition to problems that may be related to the intrinsic properties of the active ingredients, metabolites or excipients of a medicine, medically important risks may arise from accidental or intentional contamination or product defects (e.g., poisoning of Tylenol (acetaminophen/paracetamol) capsules in the United States; toxic contaminant in L-tryptophan in Japan; or inadequate potency or lack of sterility due to a manufacturing flaw). Although the cause may not be apparent at the onset of the initial signal — and therefore it may appear that a shift has occurred in the benefit-risk profile — once its source has been identified and corrective steps undertaken, a formal benefit-risk assessment may no longer be indicated.

7. Although economic considerations (e.g., cost-effectiveness) exert an increasingly pervasive influence in the choice and use of medicines within health care systems, the Working Group believes that they should not influence the types of benefit-risk assessment covered here. See D.4. (below) and Chapter IV for more discussion on this point.

8. A benefit-risk assessment is only as good as the underlying data and their treatment. Although a manufacturer may have access to most or all of the extant data on its own product, it often has difficulty obtaining comparable information on the other treatment options under consideration, particularly if the data are unpublished. Especially for medically serious conditions it is important that the concerned parties, usually companies and regulators, cooperate as much as possible and promptly exchange the needed information. Within the limits of proprietary and other confidential interests, therefore, regulators are expected to share all pertinent information with the companies concerned, toward their common goal of resolving the suspected problem. Similarly, transparency in decision-making will not only enhance the credibility of the result but also provide the experience and understanding much needed by everyone engaged in this complex undertaking (see Chapter III).

D. Factors Influencing Benefit-Risk Assessment

Even when the best and most complete data are available there can be various subjective and objective influences on the way benefit-risk is assessed, on the urgency with which the assessment is needed, and on the options for decisions and actions considered at the end of the process. The following examples cover some prominent influences on the evaluation process.

1. Stakeholders and constituencies

The main thrust of this report is to provide guidance for manufacturers and regulators, who bring a certain perspective based on their goals and responsibilities but who are ultimately acting on behalf of others. Thus, they must be aware of and sensitive to the possibly different perspectives that various stakeholders, who may weigh the information differently, bring to a benefit-risk analysis. Patients, physicians, pharmaceutical companies, ethics committees, regulatory authorities, other public health bodies, insurers, consumer groups and others may have very different perspectives[2]. This is particularly true of the relationship between benefits and risks; for example, two patients exposed to (and knowing about) the same benefits and risks may have different perceptions of, or thresholds for accepting, the risks, and thereby make different choices. An interesting analysis of this issue, with examples of the use of triazolam (a benzodiazepine hypnotic) and isotretinoin (a retinoic acid for cystic acne), has been published[6].

As discussed elsewhere in this report, it is usually advisable that some of the affected parties take part in the assessment.

2. Nature of the problem

The speed and intensity with which a benefit-risk evaluation is conducted will depend on the medical seriousness of the suspected adverse drug reaction as well as on other considerations (see 3. below). A potential threat to life, for example, clearly demands very rapid attention, with close and frequent interaction between the regulatory authorities and the company. Although the nature of a problem will usually dictate the time-course of action, it must be emphasized that all benefit-risk assessments are made in the face of uncertainty. When a major new potential safety-problem arises, the need for urgent action to protect the public from a possibly serious hazard must be weighed against the need for additional data that might provide more certainty or confidence in the analyses and conclusions (See Chapter IIE).

3. Indication for drug use and population under treatment

A drug may be used for prevention, prophylaxis or treatment and possibly for diagnostic purposes. It may be given for a life-threatening condition or a self-limiting disease; the acceptable risk for the former will undoubtedly be the higher. If it is an "orphan drug" used in limited populations or other circumstances for which there are no reasonable therapeutic alternatives the threshold for acceptable risk may be relatively high. Certain target sub-populations for the medicine may respond differently owing to ethnic differences in pharmacodynamics or pharma-cokinetics or to medical-cultural influences. Also a safety or other problem may occur in association with an unapproved (unlabelled) use.

These and other examples remind us that comparative benefit-risk analyses can be highly situational, and may be especially difficult when a single product falls into more than one of these categories (e.g., multiple indications or different dosage forms/routes of administration, with differentiable benefit-risk properties).

4. Constraints of time, data and resources

The proposals in this report call for a systematic, thorough evaluation of all available data when a signal suggests that a product carries a potentially major new risk.

As indicated above (II.C.4.), such an evaluation should take into account not only the new signal but also the overall risk profile of the product relative to that of the appropriate comparator products. In practice, especially when regulatory needs demand urgent attention (e.g., under conditions of a Type II Variation or "Urgent Safety Restriction" in the European Union), such a comprehensive, comparative benefit-risk analysis may be difficult. This is especially the case if sufficient data on comparator drugs or other modalities (e.g., surgery) cannot be obtained reasonably quickly, if the data-bases are very large (e.g., hundreds or thousands of adverse-reaction cases that might require review), and if the number of people available is limited. It would then be advisable to hold discussions with the authorities to decide on the scope and strategy of the evaluation and the written report.

5. Economic issues

Some economists have suggested that "economic efficiency" (difference between benefits and costs) should be a fundamental criterion for decisions on health and safety regulation, and have offered principles for the use of benefit-cost analyses[16] or benefit-risk-cost analyses[6]. For example, even before the widespread use of serotonin re-uptake inhibitors, Henry and Martin[17] in a benefit-risk analysis of many antidepressants counted the low cost of older drugs as part of their benefits.

---

[16] Arrow, K.J., Cropper, M.L. Eads, G.C. et al. Is there a Role for Benefit-Cost Analysis in Environmental, Health and Safety Regulation? *Science*, 272-221-222, 1996.

[17] Henry, J.A. and Martin, A.J. The Risk/Benefit Assessment of Antidepressant Drugs, *Medical Toxicology*, 2: 445-462, 1987.

Although economic impact on the allocation of medicines is receiving greater attention, the Working Group did not consider economic outcomes in terms of financial considerations in the types of benefit-risk assessment covered by this report. However, the Group did acknowledge and invoke important concepts and methods of economics science, such as trade-offs and weighings.

Once it is established that conventional benefit-risk evaluation shows no significant differences between different products, cost may be one basis for choosing among them for a patient who responds equally to them. It must also be acknowledged, however, that in economically depressed areas a medicine with a less advantageous benefit-risk balance may be the only affordable alternative. Willingness to accept risk may therefore depend on cost in many parts of the world, where health regulators and other authorities may indeed regard it as a normal aspect of decision-making.

E. The Evidence and Analytical Approaches

The treatment of benefit evaluation and risk evaluation in Chapter II includes examples of the kinds and amounts of data and their interpretation that should be brought to bear in benefit-risk assessment. Some general considerations are appropriate here, along with some discussion of combining benefit and risk metrics.

1. Information and its limitations

When a signal arises that leads to a re-evaluation of the benefit-risk profile, a manufacturer or regulator will attempt to gather as much information as possible from animal, *in vitro* and human investigations or exposure. Evidence from both empirical and non-empirical sources will usually be available. For a marketed drug, much of the data come from uncontrolled sources of surveillance (e.g., spontaneous reports) and are often factually uncertain, incomplete and imprecise.

Controlled clinical trials and observational studies provide data that are more reliable, but some caveats are indicated. A clinical-trial data-base typically available for benefit-risk evaluation is mostly the result of drug development programmes designed to demonstrate and assess efficacy. Such programmes invariably include carefully selected populations of limited size (usually below 10,000 patients); conditions are highly controlled and treatment periods relatively short; the object is to reach statistically meaningful efficacy-endpoints for the purpose of regulatory approval.

There are thus inherent limitations regarding generalizability of both efficacy and safety to "real world" populations, as well as inadequate power to detect relatively rare but potentially significant adverse reactions. These and other difficulties with randomized clinical trials have been extensively described.[18] Nevertheless, there are useful strategies for distinguishing between drug-related and non-drug-related adverse events.[19]

Structured post-marketing surveillance follow-up and ad hoc case-control studies are capable of examining larger populations in more "naturalistic" circumstances and over longer periods of drug exposure than most randomized controlled clinical trials. Some of these studies can be performed with large automated data-bases of records collected for administrative, clinical or other purposes, supplemented with other clinical records as needed, to validate exposures and diagnoses. Researchers may need to anticipate bias in the selection of patients treated in any non-randomized studies, and to design the studies and analyses carefully. However, because of their larger potential sizes and "real world" settings, these studies may represent the only opportunity to quantify the risk of a particular adverse event, to evaluate predictors of risk, and to estimate risk in populations typically excluded from clinical trials (e.g., pregnant women).

Nevertheless, such studies usually cannot provide primary evidence for causation and can indeed lead to false-positive associations.[20, 21] An excellent example of the inherent difficulties in this area is the ongoing debate about third-generation oral contraceptives and venous thrombosis.[22]

Ideally, for comparisons between treatment alternatives, like types and amounts of data should be available for all the options under consideration. In practice, this is rarely the case and there are frequent gaps in the quantity and quality of information. Moreover, in comparing pharmaceuticals with other options (e.g., surgery or other modalities) there are additional difficulties (different measurements and scales, and different medical cultures and expertise). Finally, in deriving a measure of the relationship

---

[18] Laupacis, A., Sackett, D. and Roberts, R. An Assessment of Clinically Useful Measures of the Consequences of Treatment, *New England Journal of Medicine*, 318: 1728-1734, 1988.

[19] Hsu, P.-W., Pernet, A.G., Craft, J.C. and Hursey, M.J. A method for Identifying Adverse Events Related to New Drug Treatment, *Drug Information Journal*, 26: 109-118, 1992.

[20] Feinstein, A.R. Meta-analysis: Statistical Alchemy for the 21st Century, *Journal of Clinical Epidemiology* 48: 71-78, 1995.

[21] Milloy, S. *Science Without Sense. The Risky Business of Public Health Research*, Cato Institute, Washington, DC, 1995.

[22] Hughes, S. More evidence in favor of third-generation oral contraceptives, *SCRIP*, No. 2279. October 28, 1997, p.7.

between benefits and risks, value judgments are needed for giving weight or priority to the undesirability of adverse effects (e.g., "seriousness") and to the desirability of beneficial effects. Such judgments can be highly subjective and will vary among health professionals and patients.

It is important, therefore, to obtain data from all relevant sources, to document carefully all the information, and to record the assumptions adopted and any limitations in the use of the data for analysis. If there are considerable uncertainties, such as those mentioned here, sensitivity analyses may be helpful in determining the robustness of the assessment or whether the conclusions drawn from various models differ in any significant respects.

2. Benefit-risk metrics

If the benefits of the various options under consideration can be assumed to be equal, benefit-risk evaluation can rely on measures of relative risk. Otherwise, in the absence of a readily available and quantitative relationship between benefits and risks, which is commonly the case, evaluation usually comes down to analyses and conclusions that rely on indirect, informal and unavoidably subjective processes. There are no accepted general methods for deriving a "benefit-risk ratio" or another composite metric, or for using such measures to compare relative merits of alternative treatments. As ordinarily used, therefore, the benefit-risk "ratio" compares figuratively, but not often quantitatively, the relative magnitudes of benefits and risks. Some hold that it is more meaningful to speak of benefit-risk difference, the net value a patient (or population) can expect from a therapy. Selected attempts described in the literature and some new approaches considered by the Working Group are presented in Chapter IID.

At a minimum, an attempt should be made to quantify the incidence of the event in the treated population, if possible by age, sex and other characteristics of significance for the medicine's indication.

II. STANDARD FORMAT AND CONTENT OF A BENEFIT-RISK EVALUATION REPORT

The Working Group recommends a standard outline for a written report to describe the results of a benefit-risk evaluation. The outline and check-list shown below are regarded as a reasonable approach toward such a standard for a self-contained ("stand-alone") report. The items listed are meant to provide a preview and abstract of the more fully developed themes in sections IIA through IIE, which follow the outline and which discuss the basis for the content of a report.

OUTLINE OF A REPORT

A. Introduction

- Brief specification/description of the drug and where marketed
- Indications for use, by country if there are differences
- Identification of one or more alternative therapies or modalities, including surgery
- A very brief description of the suspected or established major safety problem

B. Benefit evaluation

- Epidemiology and natural history of the target disease(s)
- Purpose of treatment (cure, prophylaxis, etc.)
- Summary of efficacy and general toleration data compared with:
  - other medical treatments
  - surgical treatment or other intervention
  - no treatment

C. Risk evaluation

- Background
- Weight of evidence for the suspected risk (incidence etc.)

- Detailed presentations and analyses of data on the new suspected risk
- Probable and possible explanations
- Preventability, predictability and reversibility of the new risk
- The issue as it relates to alternative therapies and no therapy
- Review of the complete safety profile of the drug, using diagrammatic representations when possible ("risk profiles"); when appropriate, focus on, e.g., the three most common and the three most medically serious adverse reactions
- Provide similar profiles for alternative drugs
- When possible, estimate the excess incidence of any adverse reactions known to be common to the alternatives
- When there are significant adverse reactions that are not common to the the drugs compared, highlight important differences between the drugs.

D. Benefit-risk evaluation

- Summarize the benefits as related to the seriousness of the target disease and the purpose and effectiveness of treatment
- Summarize the dominant risks (seriousness/severity, duration, incidence)
- Summarize the benefit-risk relationship, quantitatively and diagrammatically if possible, taking into account the alternative therapies or no treatment
- Provide a summary assessment and conclusion

E. Options analysis

- List all appropriate options for action
- Describe the pros and cons and likely consequences (impact analysis) of each option under consideration, taking alternative therapies into account
- If relevant, outline plans or suggestions for a study that could provide timely and important additional information
- If feasible, indicate the quality and quantity of any future evidence which would signal the need for a re-evaluation of the benefit-risk relationship
- Suggest how the consequences of the recommended action should be monitored and assessed.

A. Introduction to a Report

The introduction should briefly describe the medicine and the report in a way that ensures that reviewers will interpret correctly the scope of the document. Reference should be made not only to products covered but also to those excluded. It is also important to mention whether data are included from other parties, such as co-marketers or licensees/licensors, and whether it is known that they are preparing separate reviews.

One of the first steps in a comparative benefit-risk assessment is to specify the alternative therapeutic products. Ideally, for fair comparison, the alternatives will have the same indications and durations of treatment. Comparisons will also try to match, or at least define and account for, the severity of the disease treated even for the same indication, concomitant medications, and age and sex distribution of the affected populations. In addition to alternative medicines, the comparison could include surgery, other treatment modalities or no treatment. Thus, the therapies selected for comparative analysis should be specified, along with the rationale of their selection. It may be necessary or desirable to obtain the advance agreement of the regulatory authority on the selections.

B. Benefit Evaluation

1. Introduction

A benefit-risk analysis logically begins with a discussion of the benefits, since the beneficial effects are the basis for use of a drug or vaccine. The benefits should be described and wherever possible quantified in a way that is comparable to the quantification of risks (e.g., potential lives saved as a result of treatment vs. potential lives lost as a result of adverse reactions). Benefit (and risk) may be defined in terms of the individual being treated, of net benefits across individuals being treated or, as in the case of vaccines or antibiotics, of the net benefit to society.

The discussion of benefits should include consideration of the epidemiology and natural history of the disease being treated, the purpose or intended outcome of treatment, the evidence upon which the benefits have been established, and the availability of alternative therapies. Those points are discussed in detail below. The various points to be considered in a benefit evaluation are summarized at the end of this section.

The terms *benefit* and *efficacy* have customarily been regarded as synonyms; their expression has been derived from metrics used in clinical trials. However, this concept of benefit has been extended to embrace additional measures such as quality of life, compliance with therapy, outcomes, and the notion of "evidence-based medicine."[1] Although these metrics have so far been little used in benefit-risk analysis, such measures as quality of life are likely to become increasingly important.[2]

For illustrative purposes, and because it could be misleading to consider benefit in isolation, some of the cases described here include discussions of aspects of risk and benefit-risk (covered in more detail in II.C. and II.D., respectively).

2. Description of the epidemiology and natural history of the target disease

A description of the epidemiology and natural history of the target disease is usually helpful for putting both benefits and risks into perspective. The epidemiology may be described in terms of the incidence or prevalence of the targeted disease as well as of the specific populations at increased risk (e.g., based on age or sex, renal or hepatic insufficiency, etc.). The natural history of the disease is important for differentiating self-limiting conditions (e.g., the common cold or trauma) from chronic and progressive disease states (e.g., diabetes, coronary heart disease, cancer, AIDS) or underlying disease with intermittent acute exacerbations (e.g., asthma, multiple sclerosis, gout). Tolerance of risk will generally be much greater for therapies that change the natural history of acute or chronic conditions associated with significant morbidity or mortality (e.g., HIV disease, coronary heart disease, or osteoporosis) than for those that provide symptomatic relief in otherwise self-limiting conditions not known to be associated with significant morbidity.

The Lennox-Gastaut syndrome is a severe epileptic encephalopathy refractory to conventional treatment. In France there are 4000 new cases of epilepsy a year in children, of which 30% are resistant to therapy and 1% are severe enough to be considered Lennox-Gastaut. The cumulative annual incidence of sudden death among patients with the syndrome is 1 in 500. Felbamate (Appendix B) is an antiepileptic drug that has been found to dramatically reduce morbidity and mortality in patients with the syndrome, for whom there is no alternative drug. Felbamate is associated with severe blood dyscrasias, including aplastic anaemia. Surgery has been used

---

[1] Taubes, G. Looking for the Evidence in Medicine. *Science*, 272: 22-24, 5 April 1996.

[2] *Tools Employed in the Measurement of the Risks and Benefits of Drugs* — A Literature Review for the Canadian Public Health Association's National Panel on Risk/Benefit Management of Drugs. Curry Adams and Associates, Ottawa, Ontario, Canada, July 1991.

successfully in the treatment of the syndrome but it too carries some risk. In this example, given the life-threatening nature of the disease, it may be appropriate to use a therapy known to be associated with significant risk, as long as the risk is lower than that of any available alternative, including no intervention.

3. Purpose or intended outcome of the treatment

The threshold of acceptable risk will vary with the purpose and intended outcome of the treatment. It is important, therefore, to describe clearly its intended impact on the defined natural history of the disease being treated. From a regulatory perspective, this discussion will ordinarily be confined to the approved indications.

Tolerance for a drug-associated risk will generally be low when the drug is intended to prevent disease in an otherwise healthy person; the degree of acceptable risk will be influenced by the extent to which the disease and its associated morbidity and mortality can be prevented. Tolerance will generally be greater for a product intended to prevent serious or fatal complications of existing disease. For example, the tolerance for risk associated with cholesterol-lowering agents will be low for their use in patients without confirmed coronary heart disease, whose only risk factor may be moderately elevated serum cholesterol, but it will be somewhat higher in the case of patients with a history of myocardial infarction and at high risk of its recurrence. Since the natural history of HIV disease is such that virtually all of those infected could be expected to die of it before promising new drugs became available, the tolerance for risk associated with current drugs will be relatively high as long as there are no better alternatives.

Vaccines to prevent childhood diseases are instances of interventions in otherwise healthy populations, in which risk-tolerance will be low. The case of vaccines is unique in that the benefit-risk evaluation will generally require consideration of the societal as well as the individual perspective. Hence, the description of the benefit would have to take into account the overall effects of vaccination programmes on occurrence of disease in entire populations. Likewise, choice of antibiotics would take into account the risk of organisms becoming resistant, which would pose a risk to future patients and alter the future beneficial effects of the product.

When a safety issue is so significant that it warrants a reassessment of the benefit-risk relationship, it usually refers to a potentially life-threatening adverse reaction. Hence, in terms of comparability, benefit-risk evaluation of medicinal products intended to reduce morbidity and mortality is likely to be relatively straightforward — i.e., comparison of morbidity and mortality with and without the intervention. However, when a drug is intended to be palliative (e.g., for post-surgical pain), to relieve chronic symptoms (NSAIDs for chronic arthritis), to reduce the frequency or exacerbation of intermittent symptoms (treatment of chronic asthma), or to reduce the risk of treatable complications (post-surgical prophylactic antibiotic use), the benefits and risks are not so easily compared. In such circumstances, measures of quality of life take on greater importance.

In addition to the intended purpose or outcome, the intended place of the product in clinical practice must be made clear. Certain products may have second-line status owing to previously identified risks or limited efficacy/ effectiveness or, as in the case of some antibiotics, because their use should be curtailed to preserve their benefits for future patients by reducing the opportunity for resistance to occur. While certain risks may not be acceptable for first-line therapy when a safer product is available, the same risks may be acceptable when there is no safer or effective alternative. In the example above, felbamate is an accepted treatment for Lennox-Gastaut syndrome, where patients are by definition resistant to other drugs, but it would not be acceptable as first-line therapy in uncomplicated epilepsy.

4. Evidence for benefits: Degree of efficacy achieved in clinical trials and effectiveness in clinical practice

From a population-based perspective, and because of the societal implications, the number or proportion of deaths prevented or patients spared or cured of a disease by the drug or vaccine is of paramount importance. In general, the degree to which the product achieves such an intended outcome should be described. This would include a review of both its efficacy (effect under ideal clinical conditions) and its effectiveness (effect under usual conditions of clinical practice).

Although it is customary to express benefits of preventive therapies in terms of percentage reduction in mortality or another predefined endpoint (e.g., reduction of AIDS-related diagnoses with antiretroviral agents), such a metric can be highly misleading unless accompanied by data on the absolute values describing the treated and untreated (or active comparative) group. This is especially so when such benefit statistics are being compared with those of product-associated risks. For example, rather than state simply that a product compared with no treatment achieved a 33% reduction in the incidence of some medical event, the absolute rates for the compared groups should be given as well (e.g., a background fatality rate of 30% compared with a treated rate of 20%, which represents a 33%

reduction from the background rate or, expressed in another way, an absolute reduction of 10%). It may also be informative to describe a preventive agent in terms of the number of individuals who would need to be treated, and for how long, to prevent one morbid or fatal event.

For products intended for treatment of established disease, the measurable effect will vary according to whether the treatment results in decreased mortality, decreased morbidity, symptomatic improvement or improved quality of life. For symptomatic or palliative treatment, measurement of benefit would likely be in terms of extent and duration of symptom relief or improvement.

Often, though less commonly in recent years, drugs are approved on the basis of surrogate markers of disease and disease outcome. For example, antihypertensive agents are generally approved on the basis of clinical trials showing efficacy in terms of lowering of blood pressure rather than reduction in cardiovascular events. In this case, the effect of the drug on morbidity and mortality will be determined by epidemiological data or clinical trials of other antihypertensive agents rather than by direct evidence. Although this will generally be acceptable for long-established therapies, data from studies that directly measure the impact of a particular drug on morbidity and mortality will always be considered stronger evidence of benefit than extrapolation of results from epidemiological studies or other interventions.

Any discussion of benefits should take into account the degree to which they have been demonstrated, the degree of certainty of results of clinical trials, and the generalizability of clinical trials to the broader population targeted for treatment. If quality of life, utilities, quality-adjusted-life-years, psychosocial factors or functional status are used, the methods used to measure them and the steps taken to validate the measurements should be defined.

In the United States, quinine was available over-the-counter for treatment of nocturnal leg cramps, a relatively benign and otherwise self-limiting condition of unknown aetiology. Clinical trials did not support its efficacy: the analyses were flawed, or several confounding factors were present, or there was no demonstrable difference between quinine and placebo. Hence when it became apparent that quinine may be associated with allergic haematological events, the lack of evidence of clinical benefit was a determining factor in the decision to remove it from over-the-counter use.

5. Alternative therapies: Comparison of benefits

Included in the comparison should be a discussion of alternative therapies and their relative efficacy and effectiveness, indication by indication if there is more than one. If there is no alternative therapy, the appropriate comparison would be with no treatment or non-drug modalities or both. In this case, a particular effort should be made to understand the natural history of the disease being treated. If there are other viable alternative therapies, all of their benefits (and risks) should be compared with those of the medicine in question. The validity of any such comparison should be considered. Ideally, but unusually, one would know of clinical trials with head-to-head comparisons of all alternative therapies. Instead of direct comparisons, data should be sought from studies carried out in comparable populations and using comparable methods of data collection and analysis. Without such data, any valid comparison of therapies will be difficult. Any attempt to make such a comparison should include a discussion of the limitations and potential pitfalls of the comparative analysis.

Oral polio-vaccine is an example of a preventive product which, in the context of mass immunization, is responsible for the near eradication of polio from many developed countries. Polio is associated with significant morbidity and mortality. The live attenuated oral vaccine is more efficacious than the alternative, killed vaccine. However, the United States in recent years has had more cases of polio caused by the live attenuated vaccine than by wild polio virus. This is why the recommendations for polio vaccination have recently been changed, from a course of three doses of the live, attenuated oral vaccine to a course of two doses, followed by two doses of killed vaccine. This practice is expected to prevent half of the eight to ten cases of vaccine-induced polio annually in the United States. It is also an example of how recommendations may be changed as new information becomes available to alter the benefit-risk balance.

Temofloxacin provides an example of a drug that was used primarily to treat infections of the urinary and respiratory tracts but was removed from the market because of unacceptable risks. Such infections can be life-threatening if left untreated, especially in susceptible populations, but there are equally efficacious alternative drugs. Of course, the choice of alternative depends on its relative risk, as well as benefits, as indicated in the next section.

6. Alternative therapies: Comparison of tolerability, convenience and preference

Because it is likely to affect compliance and therefore overall effectiveness and quality of life, tolerability in relation to alternative therapies should also be discussed. Other considerations when comparing relative benefits may include route of administration (e.g., oral or subcutaneous), frequency of dosing, palatability, or other factors that relate to convenience or patient preference.

Schizophrenia is a serious chronic disease with a 1% lifetime prevalence; about half of the patients suffer chronic disablement and about 10% commit suicide. Remoxipride, an antipsychosis agent of the benzamide group, was approved in Sweden for the treatment of schizophrenia as well as other types of psychosis in which delusions, hallucinations and thought disturbances are prominent symptoms and where the classical neuroleptics have been found to cause intolerable side-effects. In clinical trials no difference in efficacy was observed between remoxipride and haloperidol, thioridazine or chlorpromazine. Shortly after its approval, remoxipride was removed from the market owing to a higher than expected incidence of aplastic anaemia. However, the general tolerability profile of remoxipride was better, with fewer drop-outs and less sedation, than that of haloperidol, and it caused less sedation and fewer autonomic side-effects than chlorpromazine or thioridazine. On this basis, some have argued that there is still a place for this drug in the treatment of schizophrenia.

7. Points to consider in evaluation of benefits — A check-list

The epidemiology and natural history of the target disease

What is the incidence/prevalence of the disease or condition?

Have any high-risk populations been identified?

Is the disease self-limiting, or fatal or disabling, or one with considerable morbidity or is the condition being treated an asymptomatic risk factor for subsequent disease?

If the condition being treated (e.g., hypercholesterolaemia or hypertension) represents a precursor or risk factor for another disease or condition (e.g., coronary heart disease or stroke), how well does the risk factor predict the occurrence of the more serious disease?

What is the potential impact (i.e., the benefit) of the therapy on the disease or risk?

If the disease itself is the direct target of treatment, what is its associated morbidity and mortality?

What is the potential impact of early intervention on the disease?

What are the consequences of no intervention?

Are there prognostic factors to be considered in relation to disease outcome?

Purpose or intended outcome of the treatment

Is the purpose of the treatment:

- to prevent disease (e.g., vaccine)?
- to prevent the recurrence of disease (e.g., antibiotic prophylaxis for otitis media)?
- to treat an acute condition (e.g., streptococcal pharyngitis)?
- to treat symptoms of a self-limiting condition (e.g., a decongestant)?
- to reduce the risk of a serious outcome (e.g., treatment of hypertension, hypercholesterolaemia or osteoporosis)?
- to prevent progression of disease (thrombolytic therapy)?
- to treat chronic disabling symptoms (e.g., NSAIDs for chronic arthritis)?
- to reduce or delay morbidity or mortality among patients (e.g., treatment of AIDS or cancer)?

Are there prognostic factors to be considered in relation to the expected response to treatment?

Is benefit more appropriately defined in terms of:

- the individual being treated
- net benefits across individuals being treated (e.g., cholesterol-lowering)
- net benefit to society (e.g., vaccines, antibiotics)?

Is the product recommended as first-line or second-line therapy (second-line when other first-line therapies have failed)?

Evidence of benefits: Degree of efficacy achieved in clinical trials and effectiveness in clinical practice

What is the evidence of efficacy (effect of the intervention under ideal clinical conditions)?

What is the evidence of effectiveness (effect of the intervention under usual conditions of clinical practice)?

For preventive agents:

- to what extent is the risk factor for the disease affected and what is the associated reduction of disease risk?

- how many would need to receive the product, and for how long, to prevent one person from experiencing a morbid or fatal event?

For disease treatment, what are the measurable effects of therapy, such as decreased mortality, decreased morbidity, symptomatic improvement, improved quality of life?

For treatment of symptoms, to what extent and for how long are symptoms improved and in what percentage of patients? Do the demonstrated effects represent only surrogate markers of disease and disease outcome (e.g., blood sugar, blood lipids)? If so, what is the evidence that the surrogate measures are valid markers?

How are beneficial effects measured, what is the quality of the available data, and what is the relevance of the measurements to outcomes that patients consider important?

What is the level of certainty in interpreting results of clinical trials?

Are the results of clinical trials generalizable to the broader population targeted for treatment?

Alternative therapies

If there is no alternative therapy, what is the effect of no treatment or a non-drug intervention? (See discussion of natural history.)

If there are other viable alternative therapies:

- are data available on comparable populations from studies utilizing comparable methods, so that the therapies may be validly compared as to efficacy and effectiveness?

- if so, how do the alternatives compare in these respects with the treatment in question?

- are there other important factors to be considered in relation to alternative therapies, such as tolerability, convenience or patient preference?

C. Risk Evaluation

1. Introduction

The benefits and risks of medicinal products are continuously evaluated during drug development. An unfavourable benefit-risk balance in the development phase usually results in cessation of research. Before marketing, clinical trials are the exclusive source of data on efficacy in humans but they also provide high-quality comparative data on the risks of the drugs being developed. Adverse reactions that are linked to the pharmacological action of a medicinal product are predictable, usually dose-dependent in a rather straightforward way, and likely to occur frequently (e.g., symptomatic hypotension during treatment of hypertension, hypoglycaemia in insulin-treated diabetic patients, or bradycardia with beta-blockers). Other adverse effects, such as allergic and idiosyncratic reactions, are neither predictable nor dose-dependent and occur mostly in persons who may have a special sensitivity.

In contrast to the benefits of medicines, usually represented as one or more than one well-defined outcome, risks usually include a mixture of adverse reactions of different types. The medical impact of an adverse reaction is characterized by its frequency of occurrence, duration and intensity. Different reactions are not comparable unless they can be expressed by a common health-outcome measure. Thus, drug-risk evaluation requires a multifactorial approach in order to determine the qualitative profiles of different adverse reactions (including the signal reaction of concern), their frequency of occurrence, and, if possible, the one or more health outcomes common to different reactions. Only such a composite approach allows a fair risk-comparison of therapeutic alternatives.

Although the quality and amount of available information on therapeutic alternatives may vary, all that is available, preferably as of a defined date, should be compiled. The absolute and relative risks are never formally analysed with total knowledge of all their parameters. It is therefore crucial that the best estimates possible be obtained from all available information by means of analytical and statistical tools appropriate to the specific circumstances. All qualitative and quantitative assumptions must be explicitly documented. Risk evaluation usually underestimates the actual risk of previously unidentified adverse reactions associated with marketed medicinal products, owing in part to underreporting. It should be updated, therefore, when sufficient new information becomes available. Cut-off dates and key words (such as medical subject headings) used in a literature search must be carefully documented.

Potentially fatal reactions such as anaphylactic shock, agranulocytosis or acute renal failure are quite rare. They have been documented as occurring in far less than 1 in 5000 patients receiving therapy. Since pre-marketing clinical trials usually include at most a few thousand subjects, they are unlikely to reveal potentially fatal adverse reactions. After approval, when medicinal products are used in much larger populations, such rare reactions may become evident. Different methods can be used for the surveillance of risks; spontaneous reports and case series from the literature have been among the most common and useful in generating signals.

Once signals are identified, the overall risk attributed to a medicinal product must be reassessed and quantified, and compared with that for its therapeutic alternatives. For this purpose, it is usually necessary to use population-based data from which to determine the incidence of expected cases over a designated observational period in a defined population of patients taking the product. The handling of such data for the evaluation of drug-attributed risks is the domain of pharmacoepidemiology. Usually when reports of such cases are first published there are no epidemiological data on the frequency of rare but potentially serious adverse reactions. Epidemiological studies are important, however, and perhaps necessary, for testing hypotheses on a new signal.

The methodology of risk evaluation is described below in terms of the basic elements and techniques that are expected to yield a reproducible and transparent quantification and description of risks attributable to drugs.

2. General Considerations in an Analysis

History and description of specific adverse drug reactions prompting the benefit-risk evaluation

It is necessary to begin with a history of how the new safety issue came to light and to follow with a thorough review of the evidence and whether the evidence is sufficient to ascribe causality. In addition to the nature, severity, associated outcome (morbidity and mortality) and duration of an event, many other factors have to be considered. They include any dependence of the temporal relationship on use of the drug (e.g., dose or duration of treatment), physico-chemical characteristics of the drug (e.g., fat solubility, protein build-up, enzyme inhibition/activity, metabolism, relationship to fast acetylation and genetic polymorphism), the possibility of a class effect, a possible effect of concomitant treatment (including the occurrence of drug-drug or other interactions), the background incidence of the event, possible correlations of such variables as demographics and concomitant diseases, and supporting evidence from clinical trials or animal studies.

Moreover, what were the circumstances under which the event became known? For example, a report of a cluster of cases, stimulated by a public notice or publication, should be put into proper perspective. In certain unusual circumstances, causes other than the chemical entity should be considered, such as when reports are inconsistent with the known safety profile of an established product, or there is an unusual lack of response to a treatment for life-threatening illness (an indirect safety issue), or there is no biologically plausible mechanism for producing the reaction. Such causes could include a defective product or foul play, including tampering with, counterfeiting or sabotaging the product. Other causes may relate to excipients, contamination or potency.

All these and other considerations relate to the strength of the evidence in assessing a signal, as described in detail in the report of CIOMS Working Group III.[1]

Finally, great care must be taken in any attempt to extrapolate the results beyond the specific populations (perhaps even geographic locations) and alternative products under consideration.

Preventability, predictability and reversibility of the reaction

Another aspect of risk evaluation relates to the events before and after a reaction occurs — in other words, the natural history of the reaction. Although this may not affect directly the determination of the risk of occurrence of an adverse reaction, it can affect the subsequent comparative analysis of overall benefit-risk among alternative therapies and must be borne in mind. How difficult is it to treat the reaction? Is it easily reversible? What are its pharmacological properties in the presence of concomitant medications or concurrent diseases? Could it have been prevented by appropriate labelling changes or education about dosing and administration? Are there early warning signs or symptoms that could signal the need to discontinue treatment, especially when it is known that this can reverse the reaction?

If signs and symptoms occur only at a late stage (e.g., in agranulocytosis), what are the prospects of detecting the reaction earlier by laboratory testing? If early detection is possible and it can improve the outcome prognosis, is it practical to maintain surveillance for the reaction? Can high-risk individuals be identified for more intense surveillance? What are the consequences of not detecting the reaction early?

---

[1] *Guidelines for Preparing Core Clinical-Safety Information on Drugs*, Report of CIOMS Working Group III, Council for International Organizations of Medical Sciences, Geneva, 1995.

Prior to the approval of remoxipride in Sweden and the United Kingdom, clinical trials had demonstrated that it had a more favourable tolerability profile than other anti-psychosis agents. About two years after the first approval it was noted that seven cases of aplastic anaemia (and one of severe thrombocytopenia — possibly early aplasia) had been reported. An estimated 50,000 patients had been treated with the drug, for an overall incidence of about one case in 6,000 (5 in 10,500 patients in the United Kingdom and 2 in 16,500 in Sweden).

Spontaneous reports indicated that the risk of fatal and other serious adverse reactions to remoxipride was probably the same as that for other neuroleptics. However, unlike the reactions associated with some alternative drugs (e.g., agranulocytosis), it is uncertain whether early detection of aplastic anaemia decreases the risk of a fatal outcome. Generally, by the time abnormalities in peripheral blood are detectable it is too late.

The concept of *risk driver* and its effect on risk profiles

The adverse reaction that dominates the overall risk profile (carries the most weight) is referred to as the *risk driver* or *dominant risk*. The existence and documentation of the risk driver may predate the new prompt (signal). For this and other reasons, therefore, in addition to the data on the reaction that prompted the risk evaluation, all other data on adverse reactions to the product should be taken into account in describing and quantifying the overall risk; this applies especially to other serious or frequent reactions. To obtain as complete a picture as possible, complete adverse-reaction profiles attributed to each therapeutic alternative should be compiled. Standard graphic displays for this purpose are suggested below. The circumstances and the perspective taken can determine whether the relative-risk evaluation might be restricted to a defined set of reactions, such as those that can be fatal or lead to hospitalization. If a risk driver can be identified, the risk evaluation may need to cover only one, two or three reactions. For example, an NSAID and dipyrone could be compared for the risks of upper-gastrointestinal bleeding, associated particularly with NSAIDs, and of agranulocytosis, with dipyrone, and the comparison could be weighted by statistics on mortality or days of hospitalization within a defined observational period.

In general, however, it is suggested that as a first step the three most often reported and the three most serious adverse reactions be chosen as representatives for the risk profile of each medicine in the comparison.

Risk evaluation across products

Typically, risk is evaluated for a single medicinal product, without reference to its therapeutic alternatives. Comparative risk evaluation, which is crucial and more relevant, is more difficult for many reasons. One is that knowledge of drug risks increases with exposure and duration of use; because therapeutic alternatives enter and penetrate the market at different times the amount of information available about them may differ. Also, much of the information on serious adverse reactions may originate from spontaneous reports, but the necessary information to determine with sufficient precision the frequency of drug-attributed risk is not readily available (for the company conducting the analysis, this may be true especially of information on comparator agents). Another reason is that different types of adverse reaction are not easily comparable when their clinical significance differs (e.g., duration and consequences). In addition, adverse reactions to medicines are only directly comparable if they can be described with the same measure of severity.

Once the comparators are chosen, the three key elements of risk assessment — qualitative description of the adverse reactions, their frequency of occurrence, and a weighting in a common unit of the relative importance of the reactions — should optimally provide numerical expressions for comparison.

3. Risk Profiles for Individual Drugs

A basic principle

As a simple and straightforward approach to the description and quantification of risks, the Working Group suggests the use of standard visual presentations of data on adverse reactions in the form of "profiles," usually as bar charts. Such profiles can be very useful for, as a preliminary step, illustrating patterns of data, from different sources, about the same or different medicines. The basis for this approach is found in previously published work[2, 3] on prescription-related profiles of adverse reactions for benefit-risk analysis. The comparison of risk profiles presented side by side for different drugs can be quite useful. The key components of such a standard are:

- a common set of elements (categories of outcomes)
- a common structure
- a common presentation of well-defined data.

[2] Speirs, C.J. Prescription-related Adverse Reaction Profiles and their Use in Risk-Benefit Analysis, in *Iatrogenic Diseases* 3rd edition, P.F. D'Arcy and J.P. Griffin, editors, Oxford University Press, 1986.

[3] Wiholm, B.E., Myrhed, M., and Ekman, E. Trends and Patterns in Adverse Drug Reactions to Non-Steroidal Anti-inflammatory Drugs Reported in Sweden. In Ramsford, K.D. and Velo, G.P., eds., *Side Effects of Anti-inflammatory Drugs*, Part 1, MTP Press, Lancaster, 1986, pp. 55-62.

Figure 1 is an example of such a display; it presents actual data from spontaneous reports on drug X.

Figure 1. Adverse-drug-reaction (ADR) Reporting Profile of Drug X. Number Of Spontaneous Reports Over A Specified Period

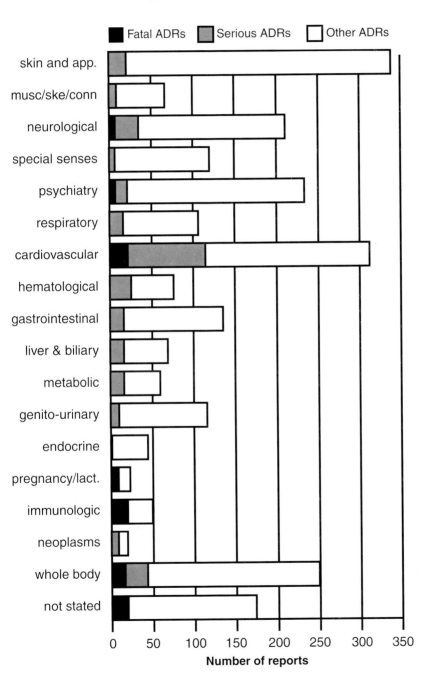

The adverse-reaction terms are sorted into body systems (system-organ classes), a widespread practice which has been proven quite useful and has been included in other proposals of the CIOMS Working Group (e.g., CIOMS III). In addition, specific reactions may be displayed in this way, grouped collectively, for example, as reactions that were serious or resulted in hospitalization or were fatal, or in other appropriate categories; profiles specific to system-organ classes may also be informative. The source of the system-organ class categories used (e.g., WHOART, COSTART, or, presumably in the future, MedDRA) needs to be specified and must not be changed, especially as system-organ classes do not necessarily comprise the same sets of preferred terms in the different terminologies now in use.

Structure and presentation of the data

It is common to sort according to estimated frequency of occurrence of adverse reactions (e.g., in order of highest to lowest, from top to bottom of the chart), and CIOMS III proposed this method in regard to core safety information. However, the sequence is likely to be different for every product. Although different sequences still permit a qualitative comparison of drug-attributed adverse-reaction profiles, it is much better to use a defined sequence, in order to establish a standard method of comparing different medicines. The sequence chosen is immaterial; it should be easy to remember and kept unchanged for the sake of familiarity and consistency, so that it is recognizable at a glance.

It is well recognized that in themselves absolute numbers of reports (as given in Figure 1) are inadequate gauges of the magnitude of reporting, especially when comparing different drugs. However, for a given drug, the distribution of reports among the different system/organ classes, or for specific adverse reactions within those classes, is very useful and can be portrayed by using percentages rather than numbers (N) of reports for each class; the numbers could still be shown on the bars if desired.

Some differentiating characteristic (e.g., colour or shading) within each bar is useful to indicate subcomponents (serious or fatal cases, for example).

For any form of presentation, such information as units, periods of time covered, and other key elements integral to interpretation of the data should be provided with the diagrams.

Specification of data sources

Profiles can be very useful for illustrating qualitative adverse-reaction reporting patterns for the same or different drugs. To avoid combining data inappropriately, separate profiles should be established for data from different sources and of different quality, such as data from spontaneous reports, clinical trials or epidemiological studies. For example, spontaneous-report data can only reflect reporting frequencies, which are influenced by many factors affecting the numerator (number of reports) and the denominator (number of drug users). Therefore, risk estimates from spontaneous reports must not be regarded as true incidences or true estimates of risk.[4]

In the absence of comprehensive information, other data sources might include official data sheets (e.g., in the European Union an updated Summary of Product Characteristics, or in the United States a package insert) or published literature; when needed, data from regulatory registries may also be available (e.g., from the US FDA via the Freedom of Information mechanism or from the Medicines Control Agency's ADROIT data-base in the United Kingdom).

Different populations (e.g., adult or paediatric), indications and dosage forms may also necessitate separate profiles. For convenient visual effect, side-by-side bar charts with negative and positive x-axes could be used to compare data from different sources.

Comparisons of profiles for different drugs

As previously discussed, only drugs with similar conditions of use and data of the same type and quality should be compared. The patterns shown in profiles are influenced by many other less obvious factors as well, which must be taken into account and discussed (e.g., proportion of new- as distinct from repeat- prescription exposures; length of time on the market; special attention given to a drug, such as "black triangle" status in the United Kingdom). When these and other influences are considered,[4] the bar-chart profiles can still be useful in demonstrating different patterns of reported observations, as in the example shown in Figure 2. A main objective of comparing profiles of different drugs is to determine which reactions for each drug should be chosen for further comparison (dominant risks).

4. Risk Weighing for Individual Adverse Drug Reactions

Ideally, for an impartial comparison of the risks associated with two or more drugs, there should be an agreed method of scoring (weighing) the

---

[4] Sachs, R. M. and Bortnichak, E. A. An Evaluation of Spontaneous Adverse Reaction Monitoring Systems, *American Journal of Medicine*, Supplement 5B, 81:49-55, 1986; Baum, S., Kweder, S. and Anello, C. The Spontaneous Reporting System in the United States, in Strom, B. L., ed., *Pharmacoepidemiology*, 2nd edition, John Wiley and Sons, 1994, pp. 125-137; and Wiholm, B., Olsson, S., Moore, N. and Wood, S. Spontaneous Reporting Systems Outside the United States, *ibid.*, pp. 139-155.)

Figure 2. Profiles of adverse reactions reported for non-steroidal anti-inflammatory drugs in Sweden (% of total reports)*

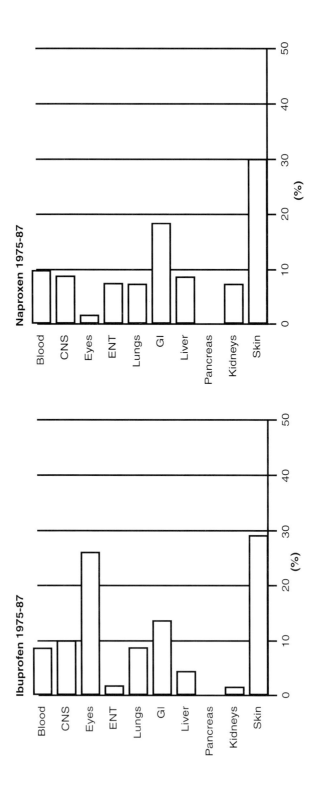

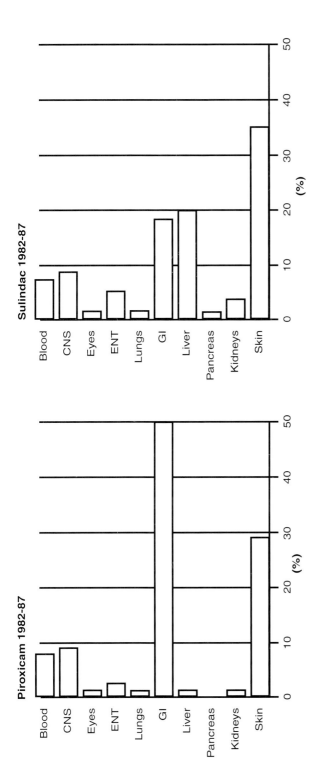

Piroxicam 1982-87

Sulindac 1982-87

* From Wiholm, B.E., Myrhed, M., and Ekman, E.Trends and Patterns in Adverse Drug Reactions to Non-Steroidal Anti-inflammatory Drugs, Part 1, Lancaster: MTP Press, pp. 55-62, 1986.

relative seriousness of different reactions. Whereas there are standard regulatory/administrative definitions for classifying a case as "serious" (death,hospitalization, etc.), little has been done on the question of how best to summarize the risks. For example, if a drug caused aplastic anaemia in 1/10,000 patients and bronchial asthma in 1/1000, how should these risks be viewed in comparison with those of a drug that caused anaphylaxis in 1/10,000, glaucoma in 1/10,000 and diarrhoea in 1/1000?

Although prescribers would like to make these kinds of comparison each time they prescribe one of a class of drugs, there is no obvious metric or method for doing so. Prescribers need to rely on their perception of risk, which is usually based on personal clinical experience. Although there is an obvious need to facilitate risk comparisons, and the Working Group was supportive of any new ideas, any method would have obvious limitations.

What methods are available? Some companies have lists of medical conditions to help them decide whether spontaneously reported cases are medically serious. The lists are often stored in a computer so that such serious cases are automatically flagged. Similarly, conditions that would always trigger an evaluation can be listed; for example, the WHO Collaborating Centre for International Drug Monitoring (Uppsala, Sweden) uses a "critical terms" list for recognizing potential signals.[5] In the future, when all companies and regulatory authorities are likely to use a single medical terminology for adverse reactions, it may be possible to assign to each preferred term a score indicating its medical seriousness, which would be useful in comparing the relative risks of drugs.

Thus, it is tempting to consider for adverse-event terms the development of a standard hierarchy or scale that would define levels of seriousness (e.g., a ranking of such conditions as anaphylaxis, myocardial infarction, gastrointestinal bleeding, rash) that could be used as the basis (threshold) for initiating a new benefit-risk evaluation and for comparing risks of alternative therapies.

In an informal test, 24 members of the Working Group scored independently 20 adverse-event terms, selected arbitrarily by one member, on a scale of 1 to 10 (10 being the most serious). The scale resulting from such an exercise obviously depends on who is doing the weighing: perspectives of patients, physicians, and others may very well differ from those of the Working Group. Table 1 shows the 20 terms ranked by their mean scores and the range of scores. Though the assessors varied in their

---

[5] *WHO Adverse Reaction Terminology — Critical Term List*, WHO Collaborating Centre for International Drug Monitoring, Uppsala, Sweden, January 1996.

opinions, adverse reactions could be broadly categorized according to the mean score into: *very serious* (score 7.5+), including aplastic anaemia, congenital abnormality, anaphylaxis, and disorders of cardiac conduction; *serious* (5-7.5), including seizures, gastrointestinal haemorrhage, asthma, glaucoma, premature labour and depression; *fairly serious* (2.5-5), including confusion, hypotension, raised liver function tests, water retention, swelling of the eyelids, urticaria, maculopapular rash, and muscle stiffness; and *least serious*, including diarrhoea and headache.

Table II shows the assessors' consistency — how reproducible the results were when 14 members of the Group repeated the scoring exercise without access to their original assessments. On average, each re-evaluated score differed by one point in either direction.

Table I: *Adverse drug reaction seriousness scores: Rank order as assessed by 24 Working Group members*

Adverse event	N	Mean	Range
Aplastic anaemia	24	9.44	6-10
Congenital abnormality	24	8.69	5-10
Anaphylaxis	24	8.10	2-10
Cardiac conduction disorder	23	7.78	4.5-10
Seizures	24	7.04	4-10
Gastrointestinal haemorrhage	24	6.63	4-10
Bronchial asthma	24	6.38	4-10
Glaucoma	24	6.00	2-8
Premature labour	23	5.65	0-8
Depression	24	5.31	3-8
Confusion	24	4.69	1-7
Hypotension	24	4.25	1-8
Raised liver function tests	23	4.15	0-7
Water retention	24	3.21	1-8
Swelling of eyelids	24	2.94	0-7
Urticaria	24	2.85	0-6
Maculopapular rash	24	2.71	0-6
Muscle stiffness	24	2.60	0-5
Diarrhoea	24	2.33	1-4
Headache	24	1.69	0-4

Overall average range   5.12   0-10

Table II: *Adverse drug reaction seriousness scores: Re-scores from 14 Working Group members*

Adverse event	New mean*	Range of change	Mean change (either direction)
Aplastic anaemia	9.57	+2 -1	0.27
Congenital abnormality	8.62	+3 -2	1.33
Anaphylaxis	8.50	+2.5-2	0.93
Cardiac conduction disorder	7.46	+2.5-3	1.18
Seizures	7.14	+2 -2	1.03
Gastrointestinal haemorrhage	6.36	+2 -3	1.00
Bronchial asthma	7.21	+4 -4	1.90
Glaucoma	5.71	+2 -3	1.03
Premature labour	4.95	+1.5-3	1.30
Depression	5.08	+2 -2	0.97
Confusion	4.96	+3 -2	1.33
Hypotension	4.48	+3 -3	1.70
Raised liver function tests	3.52	+1 -6	1.37
Water retention	2.94	+3 -2	0.93
Swelling of eyelids	3.21	+2 -2	1.07
Urticaria	3.18	+5 -2	1.13
Maculopapular rash	2.24	+1 -3	0.87
Muscle stiffness	2.87	+3 -3	1.13
Diarrhoea	2.26	+1.5-4	0.80
Headache	1.09	+1 -4.5	1.00
Overall average range	+0.05	+4 -6	1.02

* Based on 24 scores (10 scoring once and second score of the 14 scoring twice).

A similar survey conducted among a group of 221 general practitioners in the north of Yorkshire, England, ranked 63 adverse-reaction-terms in a ranking similar to that of the CIOMS Working Group.[6] Unlike the Working Group survey, however, a statistical method was used to produce a weighted index value, based on the amount of variability among the physicians. They did not repeat the exercise to test for consistency within observers.

---

[6] Kind, P. and Dolan, P. Determining the Severity of Adverse Drug Reactions: The Views of Family Doctors. A survey commissioned by Hoechst Marion Roussel. See *Proceedings of the Annual Meeting of the International Society of Technology Asssessment in Health Care* (ISTAHC), Barcelona, May 1997.

Agreed scales or values for adverse reactions would contribute to the standardization of risk quantification; the issue constitutes an important area of research. Such a system would be enhanced if duration and/or incidence of a reaction, as well as its severity, could be factored into a composite metric.

A member[7] of the Working Group has proposed a very interesting model for quantifying risks along these lines; it is presented in Appendix C to stimulate thinking and further work. It incorporates quantitative criteria for seriousness and incidence.

5. Quantification of Risk

Incidence of the reaction

To put the newly identified risk into perspective, it is important to quantify it in terms of incidence. Precise quantification will usually be difficult in the post-marketing environment, in which most new safety signals arise from spontaneous reporting, with its associated uncertainties as to numerators (reported cases) and denominators (patient exposures). However, risk can often be approximated in terms of magnitudes of 10, as suggested in the CIOMS III report: $\geq 1\%$ (common or frequent); ≥ 1 per 1000 but < 1 per cent (uncommon or infrequent); ≥ 1 per 10,000 but less than 1 per 1000 (rare); < 1 per 10,000 (very rare).

When possible, attempts should be made to determine whether the incidence is affected by the existence of any apparent high-risk groups. These might be defined by, for example, dose or duration of treatment, use of other drugs (e.g., drug interactions), presence of other diseases (e.g., renal failure), or special populations defined by demographics or ethnicity. In principle, one of the most important functions of risk evaluation is to identify individual patients at increased risk of serious adverse reactions. Although some mechanisms are fairly well understood (enzyme inhibition processes; drug interactions), the pharmacological and biological basis of drug-induced diseases (e.g., role of pharmacogenetics) is relatively unexplored. Work in this area is needed and should be encouraged.

So far, we have been referring to the "reported" (usually crude) incidence of a given adverse reaction. It is more meaningful, though, to speak of "excess incidence", namely the difference in incidence between patients exposed and not exposed to the treatment over a defined period of

---

[7] Christian Bénichou, MD, Synthélabo (Paris, France)

observation. This rate is also referred to as "drug-attributable incidence". However, "attributable" need not signify that all the cases are causally related to treatment — its meaning in this context should not be confused with its common meaning when used to ascribe causality (as in "attributable to the drug"). The incidence in unexposed patients not receiving alternative treatment (i.e., untreated) would represent the background (natural) incidence of the event in the diseased population. Calculation of excess incidence from comparative clinical trials or cohort observational studies is straightforward; in case/control studies, however, it is somewhat more complicated, as explained in standard references[8].

The next level of comparison refers to incidence relative to alternative therapies. As mentioned above, such comparative assessments of risk are more difficult, for many reasons. For example, knowledge of drug risks increases with exposure and time of use; a new drug may be associated with a relatively lower therapeutic response as well as a higher rate of adverse-reaction reporting. Thus, different timing and period of marketing, as well as extent of market penetration, influence the type and amount of information available about alternative therapies. Ideally, data for determination of comparative (as well as excess) incidence will come from clinical trials, comparative observational cohort studies, and population-based case-control studies. In the absence of such relatively high-quality data, crude estimates may be generated from other data, usually spontaneous-report statistics for different drugs during comparable post-marketing periods. It must be emphasized yet again, however, that because of the many confounders and potential biases associated with comparative spontaneous-reporting statistics[4], estimates across drugs can be misleading and great caution must be exercised in their use. It is the judgment of the CIOMS Working Group that only under exceptional and rare circumstances should the use of such comparisons form the sole basis of restrictive regulatory action.

It is also useful to keep in mind the obvious but often under-appreciated distinction between absolute and relative risk. For example, an event may occur with an excess incidence of 50%, or perhaps at an incidence 50% greater than that of a comparator. However, the meaning of such an apparently high risk can vary considerably as regards public health impact according to whether the actual incidence of an event is, for example, 1/10, 1/1000 or 1/100,000, producing an absolute excess per million patients treated of 100,000, 1000 or 10 patients, respectively.

---

[8] For example, Kelsey, J.L., Thompson, W.D. and Evans, A.S. *Methods in Observational Epidemiology*, Oxford University Press, 2nd edition, 1996, or Armitage, P. and Berry, G. *Statistical Methods in Medical Research*, Blackwell Scientific Publications, London, 2nd edition, 1987.

Two of the illustrative cases provide simple examples of incidence considerations; see Appendix B for details.

Felbamate, a drug uniquely suited to the treatment of Lennox-Gastaut syndrome, is associated with a relatively high incidence of aplastic anaemia, about 1 in 4000 patients treated (rare), with a case-fatality rate of 28% (from spontaneous reports). The evidence for causality is based on the incidence and nature of the spontaneously reported reactions. Thirty-six cases of aplastic anaemia had been reported at the time of a benefit-risk evaluation (estimated overall exposure was 120,000 patients). All had pancytopenia with severe thrombocytopenia, and most had severe bleeding and infection. Bone-marrow biopsies were consistent with aplastic anaemia. Felbamate was the only drug used in 11 cases. There were two positive rechallenges. Median time to onset was five months. There were no clear risk factors. In addition, there were 16 cases of hepatitis, of which nine were serious and fatal. Thus, total drug-induced mortality was of the order of 1/6000 patients treated. The only alternative therapy, surgery, was considered to have comparable morbidity and mortality. In contrast, the overall case fatality of untreated Lennox-Gastaut is even higher — about one in 500 cases.

Within 120 days after the introduction of temofloxacin (a fluoroquinolone) to the market in the United States, the company and the Food and Drug Administration became aware of several cases of serious adverse experiences. These included such life-threatening reactions as haemolytic anaemia, thrombocytopenia, renal impairment and hypoglycaemia. Hypoglycaemia occurred predominantly in elderly patients, but none of the other reactions was associated with a specific high-risk group. A comparison of spontaneous reports for three other fluoroquinolones did not reveal a similar problem. With estimates of patients exposed (IMS data) for denominators, the reporting rate for temofloxacin was estimated as 108 per 100,000 prescriptions, compared with 13, 25 and 20 per 100,000 for the other fluoroquinolones, and the product was subsequently taken off the market. This example highlights the observation that the usefulness of spontaneous reports increases with the severity and rarity of the adverse reaction, and when there are large apparent differences in risk between drugs.

Practical approaches to weighting adverse reactions

Only by attaching a specific weight to each adverse reaction is it possible to construct a common unit that makes it possible to qualitatively compare different reactions. As already indicated, the ideal common unit would take into account the duration, severity and consequences (outcome) of the different reactions. Depending on the circumstances, however, and in the absence of a composite standard, such markers of severity or consequence as death, life-years lost, days of hospitalization, and quality-of-life scores are examples of units that can be used when the requisite data are available. If mortality is chosen, the case fatality rate is needed. For days of hospitalization, data from diagnosis-related hospital statistics or surveys may be needed. Quality-of-life changes, days of hospitalization, or case-fatality rates are often country-specific, and this must be considered in the analysis and interpretation of the data.

Estimated total drug risk

Once one or more standard units are selected as markers for comparison (such as case-fatality rate or days of hospitalization), the weighted excess incidence rate can be calculated for each reaction by multiplying the excess incidence rate by the reaction-specific weight factor.

To obtain the weighted overall excess incidence of the combined adverse reactions associated with a particular drug, the sum of the individual values provides an aggregate (e.g., for the three most serious reactions, if this is the model chosen for comparative analysis). The chosen comparators can thus be compared on a common basis.

Finally, to obtain the incremental drug-attributable risk, the aggregate values for each drug must be subtracted from those of an arbitrary reference standard drug. The net risk corresponds to the magnitude of the incremental drug risk. For a practical example, see Appendix D.

Validity of the estimates

To test the robustness of the risk estimation, sensitivity analysis can be performed by including the precision of the risk or weighting measure. For example, if excess incidence estimates vary across studies, the lowest and highest estimates could be included in the sensitivity analysis. This procedure will provide information on the strength of the overall comparative assessment — i.e., the extent to which the overall results vary by the range of risk estimates or other assumptions.

Great care must also be taken in any attempt to extrapolate the results beyond the specific populations (including geographic locations) and treatment alternatives under consideration. If total risk estimates are extrapolated beyond the specific population from which the results originated, then all assumptions must be stated.

6. Suggested Sequential Overall Approach

On the basis of the concepts and processes described above for arriving at a fair comparison of the risks associated with competing alternative therapies, the Working Group suggests the following general methodological approach for the evaluation of drug-attributed risks. It is designed to minimize the potential for bias in the evaluation of risk and to make transparent the methods used.

(a) Define the perspective of the risk evaluation (e.g., consumer, health authority, pharmaceutical firm, public health). In the present context, this is usually a public-health perspective.

(b) Review the relevant indication and use in the target population for the subject drug (to include recommended dose, duration, age group, etc.).

(c) Specify comparator drugs (i.e., drugs that could replace the drug of interest) and alternative therapies or the no-treatment option. Provide all pertinent information as in (b).

(d) Determine and display the profile of adverse reactions for the subject drug and the specified alternatives. Risk evaluation should not be restricted to one reaction; initially, profiles should represent all reactions, but detailed analysis may be limited to a subset, especially if a dominant risk (risk driver) can be identified.

(e) Obtain the background incidence of each reaction, usually from the literature, and for each drug select the reactions with the greatest contribution to the overall risk (dominant risks). These can form part of the subset for detailed analysis (e.g., the three most serious and the three most common reactions).

(f) For the specific reactions define a common outcome measure and determine values.

(g) Estimate the excess incidence of each reaction for each therapy; drug-attributable incidence rates are the relevant risk measure.

(h) To permit comparison across reactions, adjust the excess incidence of each reaction with the weighting factor to provide the estimated weighted excess incidence rate of each reaction.

(i) Sum the weighted excess-incidence rates across reactions for each therapy to obtain the total drug-attributed risk for each treatment.

(j) Calculate the net difference between drug-attributed risks to provide a measure of incremental drug-risk relative to one of the alternatives chosen as an arbitrary reference.

(k) Ascertain the validity of the results by performing a sensitivity analysis, especially with the risk driver. Consider extrapolation of the results from the data used in the analysis to the total target population.

(l) Update the evaluation when relevant new information becomes available — from published studies, for example. Risk evaluation is a continuing process and additional data or new reactions may come to light as the number of patients using a drug increases.

The dipyrone case illustrates many of the concepts and steps discussed above (see Appendices B and D for details). In summary, the drug has been associated with agranulocytosis since the first case was reported in 1935. Evidence of causality was based on the incidence and nature of the reported events as well as on the observation of cross-sensitivity with aminopyrine, another drug known to be associated with agranulocytosis. The International Agranulocytosis and Aplastic Anaemia Study (IAAS), a large, multi-country, population-based case-control study, reported an overall annual incidence of community-acquired agranulocytosis of 3.4 per million, with a fatality rate of 10%. The excess incidence of mortality for dipyrone was 0.10 per million short-term users a week. The combined excess incidence of mortality for agranulocytosis, aplastic anaemia, anaphylaxis and serious upper-gastrointestinal complications was 0.11 per million a week for dipyrone, with gastrointestinal bleeding accounting for 69% (i.e., the dominant risk). For NSAIDs, however, the mortality per million users a week was 1.66 for aspirin, 1.50 for diclofenac and 0.43 for ibuprofen; for these drugs, serious gastrointestinal bleeding contributed 99% of the excess mortality. Agranulocytosis, the reaction that triggered the benefit-risk evaluation in this case, is associated with significant morbidity and mortality, though less so than before modern antibiotics became available. However, when mortality due to other types of adverse drug reaction is taken into account, the risk associated with many alternatives to dipyrone is considered to be as high or higher.

D. Benefit-Risk Evaluation

1. Introduction

Evaluation of benefits (Chapter IIB) and risks (Chapter IIC) for a single therapy is only apparently a simple matter; when it refers to various therapies it is particularly difficult. In general, the net benefit-risk profile for society must reflect not only how many patients are expected to benefit from a therapy and to what extent, but also the uncertainties associated with its benefits and risks. Ideally, the relationship between benefits and risks can be demonstrated by a simple graph (Figure 1). It indicates that at the extremes (high risk, low benefit; low risk, high benefit) judgments are relatively easy but that between the extremes there is more uncertainty, and decision-making can be more complex and difficult.

Rawlins[1] has classified benefit-risk assessments as formal, comparative and informal (judgmental) analyses. Formal analysis is a scientifically-deductive process, requiring quantitative comparisons of benefits and risks; the comparisons provide a numerical expression of the trade-off. An informal analysis is an inductive or subjective process, calling for personal judgment in assessing the relevant data on therapeutic options. Formal analyses, especially in recent times, have incorporated quantitative models based on studies of cost-effectiveness, cost-benefit and cost-utility, as well as the tools of meta-analysis and of decision-analysis theory.

For many benefit-risk assessments, however, neither the benefits nor the risks are easily or appropriately compared quantitatively (e.g., a drug for symptomatic relief of a common, self-limited disease but with an associated risk of a rare, life-threatening adverse reaction). In such cases, the final assessment will be largely qualitative, even somewhat subjective; the level of risk tolerance is directly related to the perceived degree of clinical benefit.

The comparative method compares qualitatively the product in question with similar products to determine whether the benefits and risks appear similar. However, the data and standards for benefit-risk assessment on the "similar," usually older, drugs may not be satisfactory by today's standards.

In informal analysis, judgment can be influenced by perceptions and standards of medical practice, including different moral attitudes and other intangible considerations. Probably most benefit-risk decisions have been made on a relatively informal basis, which has led Rawlins[1] to state that "invariably risk-benefit assessment is based on the fallibility of human judgement."

The Working Group believes, however, that the better approaches available today should be pursued; this chapter discusses various attempts described in the literature and some new techniques. Although it may not yet be possible to truly quantify a benefit-risk relationship, certain tools can strengthen the analysis and reduce reliance on judgment alone. Details of some approaches are presented in Appendix D.

---

[1] Rawlins, M.D. Risk-Benefit Decisions in Licensing Changes, in *Medicines and Risk/Benefit Decisions*, Editors S.R. Walker and A.W. Asscher, MTP Press Limited, Lancaster, 1987, pp.137-141.

Figure 1: The Benefit-Risk Spectrum

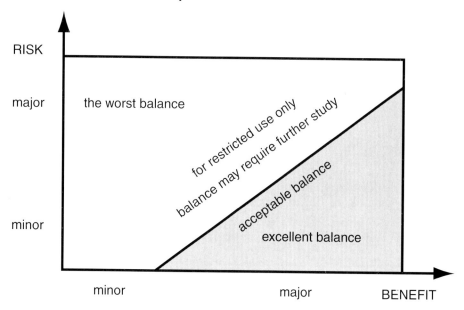

* Courtesy of W.Amery, personal correspondance

A serious obstacle to the use of a composite metric for a quantitative analysis is that benefits and risks are usually measured and expressed by different units and parameters. Besides, benefits reflect the degree to which a product decreases the risks associated with a disease; thus, it evinces a "risk-risk" dichotomy. Various attempts have been made to derive a summary statistic, mostly in the context of clinical trials. A simple example is the global assessment given by a treating physician to reflect a patient's overall response to treatment; this is commonly used in trials in Japan (referred to as *yuyosei*).[2]

In their evaluation of mass chest X-ray programmes, Payne and Loken[3] defined a benefit-risk ratio as the number of efficacy events needed for each occurrence of a serious adverse event. From 40 million X-rays, 39,250 cases of curable tuberculosis, lung cancer, leukaemia and other diseases were detected but also 723 somatic or genetic deaths, or a benefit-risk ratio of about 50:1. Chang and Fineberg[4] investigated treatment strategies in the use

---

[2] Sakuma, A. Subjectivity in Clinical Medicine, Abstracts, Drug Information Association Second Annual Biostatistics Meeting, Tokyo, Japan, August 30, 1995.

[3] Payne, J.T. and Loken, M.K. A Survey of the Benefits and Risks in the Practice of Radiology, CRC Critical Reviews in *Clinical Radiology and Nuclear Medicine*, 6: 425-439, 1975.

[4] Chang, R.W. and Fineberg, H.V. Risk-Benefit Considerations in the Management of Polymyalgia, *Medical Decision Making*, 3: 459-475, 1983.

of potentially toxic doses of steroids to control blindness in patients with polymyalgia rheumatica syndrome. They constructed an "incremental benefit-risk ratio", which represented the number of additional cases of severe toxicity for each case of blindness averted in changing from one strategy to another. In another approach, from available data on dose-benefit (dose-response) and dose-injury relationships, Andrews[5] used fitted curves to search for the optimum radiotherapeutic dose for patients with cancer.

In addition to the conventional measures of efficacy (morbidity and mortality under "ideal" conditions) and effectiveness (under more ordinary conditions), other potential influences of medicines may be considered: quality and quantity of life (e.g., quality-adjusted life-years, or QALY) and use of health-care resources (cost efficiency). As mentioned above, these are examples of metrics that can lead to more formal quantitative approaches, particularly when used in conjunction with estimations of utility values for states of health. There have been several instances of the application of multi-attribute utility-function approaches in weighing benefits and risks.[6,7] However, as the Working Group has stressed elsewhere (Chapters 1 and 7), although measurements of quality and quantity of life and economic evaluation are being used increasingly in the licensing and use of drugs[8,9], there is no agreement on what constitutes proper methods in benefit-risk assessment. Therefore, until techniques for such formal quantitative approaches are tested, standardized and validated for a number of diseases and populations, their application is limited, particularly in the present context.

However, such difficulties should not be deterrents to the use of various quantitative or semi-quantitative techniques. Some general approaches are described here to stimulate more thinking and needed research in this nascent area. Like most quantitative models, their sensitivity, reproducibility and applicability depend heavily on the "weights" or "scores" applied to the various measures of benefit and risk; such models must evolve and be

[5] Andrews, J.R. Benefit, Risk and Optimization by ROC Analysis in Cancer Radiotherapy, *International Journal of Radiation Oncology, Biology and Physics*, 11: 1557-1562, 1985.

[6] Eriksen, S. and Keller, L.R. A multiattribute-utility-function Approach to Weighing the Risks and Benefits of Pharmaceutical Agents, *Medical Decision Making*, 13:, 118-125, 1993.

[7] Schumaker, G.E. Multiattribute Evaluation in Formulary Decision Making as Applied to Calcium-channel Blockers, *American Journal of Hospital Pharmacists*, 48: 301-306, 1991.

[8] *Benefit, Risk and Cost Management of Drugs*. Report of the CPHA National Advisory Panel on Risk/Benefit Management of Drugs. Canadian Public Health Association, Janaury 1993.

[9] *Tools Employed in the Measurement of the Risks and Benefits of Drugs* — A Literature Review for the Canadian Public Health Association's National Panel on Risk/Benefit Management of Drugs. Curry Adams and Associates, Ottawa, Ontario, Canada, July 1991.

tested by collaboration of experts from health authorities, manufacturers and others.

Irrespective of method of analysis, some basic principles and approaches must be considered for a sound benefit-risk evaluation.

All available relevant data on benefits and risks should be assembled and considered for all the therapies compared.

Whenever possible, use the same, or at least comparable, parameters and outcome measures for all the therapies.

Indicate clearly all assumptions and rules adopted regarding inclusion or exclusion of data and their use, and include discussion on any value judgments in weighing the merits of different sources and types of data.

Any quantitative or qualitative model should be regarded as providing a measure of the "intrinsic" property of the medicine, reflecting for a given medicine the benefit-risk relationship at the population level.

It is useful to remember, however, that the results as applied in practice must be tempered by "extrinsic" factors, or patient characteristics, which may not be fully understood but can influence the therapeutic value of a medicine to an individual, such as[10]:

Are high responders at more or less risk than patients achieving lower degrees of benefit?

Is the patient resistant to alternative therapies and, therefore, "must" have the subject drug?

Are there factors that put a particular patient at higher or lower risk of an adverse reaction and that are not necessarily described in prescribing information?

How sensitive is the degree of risk to the needed duration of therapy (e.g., a few or many weeks)?

2. Descriptive and Semi-Quantitative Methods of Analysis

Benefits and risks can be described in relation to the intensity (seriousness or severity) of the treated disease or adverse reaction, its duration or chronicity, and, especially in the case of a reaction, its incidence in the treated population.

---

[10] Dr. W. Amery, private communication.

Thus, adverse reactions are characterized by their:

- seriousness
- duration
- incidence

Benefits may be evaluated and described for a target disease in the light of its:

- seriousness
- chronicity (e.g., acute, chronic, or duration of disease)
- extent of control or cure.

Because, presumably, all treated patients have the disease in question (thus, "incidence" is 100%), the incidence metric for adverse reactions does not apply directly to benefits in this context, *except* for the use of a drug in prophylaxis or vaccination (what is the incidence of disease with and without treatment?).

On another level, however, it may be appropriate in context to describe a disease in terms of its incidence in the population as a whole (e.g., numerically as rate of occurrence per 100,000 people per unit of time). In a simplified approach to weighing of benefits and risks, various metrics and displays summarizing comparative-benefit and comparative-risk data along the above lines can be examined informally and judgments made regarding the relative merits of alternative therapies. The challenge is to categorize the information in a way that reduces the statistics to summary proxies.

One way to reduce the complexity of an overall analysis is to express for each medicine its benefits and risks in terms of the above descriptors, and to focus on the selected adverse reactions, including the signal-generating event. If needed, benefits may also be expressed separately for each of a drug's indications. A comparison with background (no treatment) is also possible.

A number of drugs may be associated with the same or multiple different adverse reactions of different severity and frequency. Moreover, the signal event leading to a new benefit-risk evaluation may occur when the data sheet already contains a more "serious" adverse reaction recognized as the dominant risk ("risk -driver") in the overall risk profile. Also, it is likely that there is better evidence for causality and actual incidence of the most common and serious reactions.

Therefore, to make a fair comparison of risks between therapies, the "principle of threes" can accommodate most situations: choose the three most serious and three most frequent adverse reactions for each drug in the comparison.

For purposes of verbally describing benefit and risk properties, the following graduated terms are examples that could be used to describe either the disease (seriousness, duration) under treatment or an adverse reaction (seriousness, duration, incidence):

Property	High	Medium	Low
Seriousness	Fatal	Disabling	Inconvenient
Duration	Permanent	Persistent (long-lasting)	Temporary (short-lived)
Incidence	Common (frequent)	Infrequent (occasional)	Rare

To aid in reconciling the relationship between the risk and the treated disease, a tabulation of the grades is informative. A hypothetical example is shown for chronic bronchitis treated with an antibiotic that causes a medically unimportant but fairly common reaction; the disease, its alteration by the antibiotic, and the nature of the adverse reaction are depicted separately:

Nature of the disease (chronic bronchitis)

Property	High	Medium	Low
Seriousness		X	
Duration	X		
Incidence		X	

Effects of the drug on the disease

Property	High	Medium	Low
Seriousness		X	
Duration			X
Incidence*			X

* Medicines used for prophylaxis will have a score in this row. Antibiotics have an important effect on acute attacks, but less effect on the chronic course.

Adverse drug effects

Property	High	Medium	Low
Seriousness			X
Duration			X
Incidence		X	

Especially when comparing drugs, this descriptive approach cannot take into account the possibly varying types and quality of data used as the basis for filling the cells of the cross-tabulation. Obviously, judgement is needed in the categorization scheme, but it is suggested that the conceptual framework may be used as a simple, albeit crude, algorithm to maintain a consistent logic in benefit-risk evaluation. It can also contribute to more transparency in decision-making. This approach has been presented previously.[11] To illustrate its applicability, the classification grid has been applied retroactively to some of the illustrative case examples (Appendix B); a numerical scale is used for the qualitative terms (low = 1, medium = 2, high = 3; no effect/no influence = 0).

Felbamate

Aplastic anaemia is the dominant risk for felbamate, an anti-epileptic drug, which is the only effective treatment for Lennox-Gastaut epilepsy, a disease with a high mortality: 1 in 500 (seriousness score at least 2, probably 3). It is also intractable (duration 3) and rare (400 cases a year in France; incidence 1). The drug reduces dramatically the morbidity and mortality of Lennox-Gastaut epilepsy (disease seriousness reduction/ effectiveness score 3, and duration 3). Felbamate has no influence on the incidence of the disease (score 0), since it suppresses rather than prevents or cures it. More value judgement has been used in scoring the effectiveness of the drug than in scoring the disease parameters because of the limited information given in the case description.

Blood dyscrasia with aplastic anaemia "drives" the risk profile (seriousness score 3, as aplasia is often fatal); the condition is generally persistent (score 2) and the incidence is estimated at 1 in 4000 treated patients (score 2). Some might give incidence a score of 3, since the "acceptable" incidence for serious adverse reactions is often perceived as being very small compared with disease incidence. The results are easily displayed on a grid:

---

[11] Edwards, I.R., Wiholm, B.E., and Martinez, C. Concepts in Risk-Benefit Assessment, *Drug Safety*, 15 (1): 1-7, 1996.

Felbamate

	Disease	Effectiveness of the drug	Dominant reaction
Seriousness	3	3	3
Duration	3	3	3
Incidence	1	0	2
TOTAL	7	6	8

3 = high, 2 = medium, 1 = low, 0 = no effect/influence

This shows simply and clearly how the assessor has judged the effect of felbamate in a serious disease, and that the dominant adverse-reaction risk profile is marginally worse than the disease, but only in incidence. In this particular case, for a disease with no other effective treatment, the absolute comparison of benefits and risks led to the conclusion that such an effective drug as felbamate could be used for this special population but was not suitable for the general treatment of epilepsy.

Obviously, a certain amount of value judgement is needed to produce the grid scores; it is expected that as more quantitative information becomes available there will be less need of value-weighing. Nevertheless, with such an approach it should be clear that small changes in scores limited to a range of 0 to 3 may give quite different results, and the sensitivity to such changes in values must be taken into account. A broader range of scores to allow for finer differentiation can be an advantage (see TURBO model, below).

Dipyrone

For this mild analgesic, agranulocytosis is considered the dominant risk. As the dipyrone grid shows, with this simplified approach the scores

Dipyrone

	Disease	Effectiveness of the drug	Dominant reaction
Seriousness	1	3	3
Duration	1	3	2
Incidence	3	0	1
TOTAL	5	6	6

3 = high, 2 = medium, 1 = low, 0 = no effect

do not allow an obvious judgment to be made regarding the balance between effects of the disease and the particular adverse drug reaction.

However, it is useful to examine a typical NSAID, say aspirin, to demonstrate the importance of comparisons before reaching conclusions or making decisions. Aspirin is also a mild analgesic comparable in efficacy to dipyrone but with a very different dominant risk: gastrointestinal bleeding.

Aspirin

	Disease	Effectiveness of the drug	Dominant reaction
Seriousness	1	3	3
Duration	1	3	2
Incidence	3	0	2
TOTAL	5	6	7

3 = high, 2 = medium, 1 = low, 0 = no effect

The higher incidence of gastrointestinal bleeding associated with aspirin, and degree of seriousness and duration of illness similar to those of agranulocytosis, possibly give dipyrone a better risk profile than aspirin!

Quinine

Formerly used to treat leg cramps, quinine is associated with thrombocytopenia(thr) and arrhythmia(arr) as risk-drivers. This example demonstrates the presentation of data when there is more than one risk factor. Note that a sensitivity analysis can be done by weighting to some extent the seriousness of either reaction.

Quinine

	Disease	Effectiveness of the drug	Reactions
Seriousness	1	1 (or 0)	2 (thr), 1 (arr)
Duration	1	1 (or 0)	2 (thr), 1 (arr)
Incidence	2	0	1 (thr), 1 (arr)
TOTAL	4	2 (or 0)	4.0 (mean)

3 = high, 2 = medium, 1 = low, 0 = no effect

The lack of convincing efficacy data had shown that quinine was an ineffective drug for this relatively trivial condition. Even with the comparatively low scores for the adverse reactions for this indication, the benefit-risk balance is unfavourable.

It is worth emphasizing again that, for each parameter in the grid, the quantitative detail and the qualitative judgements should be described clearly. Instead of the simple grading used here, more refined numerical scores could be used, and even weighted. However, the scheme and methodology must be thoroughly documented and explained. A focus on the three most serious and three most frequent reactions for the subject drug and comparators, as already suggested, can be accommodated. The different medical options may be compared by inspecting the grids for the various adverse reactions (and benefits), or the scores may be added across each drug and the totals compared to provide a crude relative ranking.

3. Quantitative Approaches

When sufficient data on both benefits and risks are available, a more quantified version of the descriptive grid technique discussed in the previous section could be useful. In accordance with the "principle of threes" for adverse reactions, the following example illustrates the proposed method:

Drug:	Antibiotic
Efficacy:	40% cure rate for acute-on-chronic bronchitis (a disabling disease)
Adverse reactions:	Skin rash (in 20% of treated patients; lasts about three days after drug is stopped); stomach upset (in 10%; lasts up to one day afterwards); diarrhoea (in 5% of cases; may last up to three weeks afterwards and is prostrating in 0.05% of cases); agranulocytosis (in 0.005%, with 10% fatality).

For ranking (scoring) the benefit and risk properties, a convenient (but arbitrary) gradation can be chosen, similar to that used in the grid exercise (in this case, low = 10, medium = 20, high = 30). Scores are then calculated as follows, with the judgmental values shown:

Benefit score = cure rate x seriousness of the disease x chronicity/duration of the disease
= 0.4 x 30 (disabling disease) x 20 (acute-on-chronic)
= 240

Common adverse reactions (Mean score 13.3)

Skin-rash score $\quad = \quad$ 0.2 x 10 ("low" seriousness) x 10 ("low" duration) $= 20$

Stomach-upset score $\quad = \quad$ 0.1 x 10 x 10 $= 10$

Diarrhoea score $\quad = \quad$ 0.05 x 10 x 20 $= 10$

Rare adverse reactions (Mean score 0.078)

Prostrating diarrhoea score $\quad = \quad$ 0.0005 x 20 x 20 $= 0.2$

Agranulocytosis score $\quad = \quad$ 0.00005 x 30 x 20 $= 0.03$

Fatal agranulocytosis score $\quad = \quad$ 0.000005 x 30 x 30 $= 0.0045$

An overall "benefit-risk ratio" (B/R) can be calculated by using the mean of all adverse-reaction scores [(13.3 + 0.078) /2 $=$ 6.69]:
B/R $=$ 240/6.69 $=$ 35.9

Alternatively, especially to compare two or more drugs, separate B/R values for common and rare reactions could be calculated (respectively, 240/ 13.3 or 18, and 240/0.078 or 3077); individual reactions may also be compared in this way between drugs. Although it is contrary to expectation that the B/R for rare serious reactions is the greater value in the example given (a consequence of the scales chosen and the arithmetic), comparison between drugs is the key process.

Obviously, this technique is highly dependent on the scales and weightings used and it requires testing. Further development could incorporate such benefit metrics as mortality rates (measure of lives saved or deaths postponed), years of life gained, and quality-adjusted-life years (QALYs) gained; risk metrics, such as drug-attributed loss of quality-adjusted-life-years (DALQALYs), may also be applied.

For a drug-specific actual example incorporating global excess mortality risk as the principal metric, see Appendix D, which describes the benefit-risk evaluation of dipyrone compared with that of four other drugs and four different medically serious adverse reactions.

The TURBO model

A similar quantitative and graphical approach to comparative benefit-risk analysis has been proposed by Dr Willem Amery, which he calls the

TURBO model (Transparent Uniform Risk/Benefit Overview).[12] Scores are assigned to the risks (R-Score) and the benefits (B-Score) and are then combined into an overall TURBO or "therapeutic" score; the score can be regarded as a measure of the "intrinsic" property of a drug, reflecting the benefit-risk relationship at the population level for a given medication; different indications can, of course, be associated with different benefit-risk balances, usually because of different associated benefits. The ultimate goal is to place each drug in the benefit-risk spectrum (Figure 1) by use of the derived scores. See Appendix E for details.

4. General recommendations

It is recognized in regard to benefit-risk evaluation that there is no structured and harmonized approach that could serve as a standard. Techniques suggested here and elsewhere require extensive development and testing. Particular attention should be paid to the approaches outlined in Appendices D and E. However, there are some general lessons to be shared in the form of "dos and don'ts" when attempting to put the results of a benefit-risk evaluation into proper perspective.

(a) Avoid the expression "benefit-risk ratio". Until adequate quantitative approaches are validated, the term conveys a misleading mathematical credibility and has little meaning relative to impact on the public health.

(b) Avoid the use of *relative* expressions of benefits and risks in isolation; they do not reflect the true medical impact, which is better expressed in absolute values. For example, a 33% relative risk reduction may mean a decrease from an incidence of 30% to 20%, or 3% to 2%, or 0.3% to 0.2%.

(c) Be wary of uncritical use of *overall* expression of risk or benefit. Benefit and risk are rarely evenly distributed over time, the population treated, or the use of a drug (e.g., indication- or dose-dependency).

(d) Always frame the issue and the results in the proper therapeutic context, as in the following examples:

- treatment of a fatal disease with drugs that can cause fatal adverse reactions (e.g., treatment of acute leukaemia).

---

[12] The CIOMS Working Group is grateful to Dr Amery for sharing his ideas, as yet unpublished. He welcomes comments and suggestions to aid in further development and testing of the concepts presented here. (Janssen Research Foundation, Turnhoutsweg 30, B-2340 Beerse, Belgium).

- prevention of a serious, possibly fatal, condition vs. risk of a serious, possibly fatal, adverse reaction (aspirin or ticlopidine in stroke prevention vs. risk of gastrointestinal or cerebrovascular haemorrhage or, in the case of ticlopidine, agranulocytosis)
- palliative treatment that improves quality of life vs. a serious, sometimes fatal reaction (disease-modifying anti-rheumatic drugs in rheumatoid arthritis)
- relief of symptoms in non-fatal, acute, self-limiting disease (aspirin for "flu", with risk of gastrointestinal bleeding; "cure worse than the disease?")
- prevention of risks to an individual or others, as in vaccination (e.g., children vaccinated against rubella to protect pregnant women).

Finally, it is worth reiterating that the development of properly validated quantitative models for comparative benefit-risk evaluation is in its infancy and decisions are being made on a relatively informal basis. However, the semi-quantitative and quantitative methods described can add a straightforward descriptive and transparent approach to the assessment of the relative merits of different therapies.

E. Options Analysis

Introduction

To the extent possible, the risks and benefits of a medicinal product are assessed within the time-frame set by a company or regulatory authority. After a thorough assessment, all the options available should be carefully considered (options analysis) and decisions on the actions to be taken should follow. The aim is to optimize the use of the product by maximizing its benefits and minimizing newly detected risks.

The options available to regulators and manufacturers are similar but not necessarily identical, and they are not mutually exclusive; they are:

- maintenance of the status quo (i.e., no change)
- "watching and waiting" (i.e., monitoring subsequent experience)
- intensive additional data-gathering/new research (clinical or non-clinical)
- modifications to the product or its use or to the product information
- restriction of product availability

- suspension of product licence or investigational-status approval
- withdrawal of the product from the market (voluntary by marketing authorization holder or mandatory by authorities)
- communication of new or reinforced information to the medical profession or the public

Clearly, the options and decisions of a manufacturer and of a regulatory agency are interrelated and interdependent. In either case, whenever possible, the pros and cons of each option should be described in the context of the specific situation, including an impact analysis outlining the expected consequences of adopting one or other option.

Each option is now discussed in detail.

1. Maintenance of the status quo

If review of the evidence indicates no ground for concern — i.e., the suspicion of a problem raised by the original signal is unfounded — no change is warranted in the dissemination and use of the product.

2. Watching and waiting

If there is insufficient information for a definitive determination of whether there has been a change in the benefit — risk balance, the regulator may choose not to require immediate corrective action but, rather, with the manufacturer to monitor carefully the continued use of the product. It may also be prudent for the manufacturer to gather additional data for periodic review, analysis and submission.

3. Intensive additional data gathering/initiation of new research

When a potential safety problem has been identified, the manufacturer will gather and assess as much data as possible to make the best possible benefit-risk evaluation. A decision may be needed on whether obtaining additional data would help in the evaluation. The practicality of obtaining such data depends partly on how long it would take to gather the additional information, and on the nature and magnitude of the safety concern (whether it represents a potential imminent hazard to the users, for example). With these points in mind, the manufacturer should consider whether additional studies (clinical and non-clinical), additional cases of a particular adverse event, comparative data on drugs of similar therapeutic use or pharmacological class, or additional expert opinion would help in determining the benefit-risk balance. In the temofloxacin and dipyrone examples, additional comparative safety data were gathered to examine the relative risks of safety problems with the fluoroquinolone and analgesic drug classes, respectively.

Circumstances will determine whether other, parallel, action may be needed pending the results of the new research.

4. Modifications to the product or its use or to the product information

A regulatory agency and the manufacturer may introduce variations that could include changes to the prescriber or consumer information (data sheets, etc.), restriction of product use or supply, and formulation/manufacturing changes.

Changes to prescriber or consumer information

The types of product information change which might be considered include: the addition of new risk information to the sections covering ADRs, contraindications, warnings, precautions or interactions; changes in wording or emphasis to clarify or further specify adverse reactions; and restriction of indications, or in some cases, removal of information. The felbamate case illustrates restriction of indications as a means of maintaining a product on the market while attempting to limit the risk of important adverse reactions in a particularly susceptible population.

In certain cases, it may be appropriate to add a therapeutic recommendation for treating adverse reactions associated with the product.

The specific changes in product information for professionals or patients will invariably be a joint decision of regulators and manufacturers. As with any changes, the new information should be placed and worded so as to maximize understanding by health professionals and any desired changes in prescribing habits.

Restriction of product use and supply

Selective restriction of the availability of a product is sometimes considered an option to reduce the risk of an adverse reaction and to monitor safety more efficiently. For example, the placement of a drug on a narcotics scheduling list is often considered in the case of products with significant potential for abuse. In the case of quinine the Food and Drug Administration considered (but rejected) reclassifiying it from non-prescription to prescription status. Options available in some European countries, as well as in the USA under certain circumstances, include restriction of product distribution to hospitals or other specific institutions (institutional selectivity) and restriction of prescribing to specialists in the field (professional selectivity). Such options were considered in the case of felbamate in the European Union.

An option for investigational products that have a major safety problem and that have been licensed but not yet marketed is to limit distribution to patients enrolled in a "monitored release" programme (Europe) or in a compassionate use/named patient programme (North America/Europe), or to patients who have signed an informed-consent document. The latter has been used as well for a product already on the market (see the felbamate and clozapine cases).

In some countries the cost of medications is fully reimbursed by a national health-insurance plan. Some regulatory agencies can impose limits on reimbursement in order to restrict product use to a particular patient population or to limit its duration.

Changes in formulation or in manufacturing

It may be necessary or advisable to change the formulation or appearance of a product or the manufacturing process so as to minimize or eliminate an identified risk (or a reduced benefit) related to the physico-chemical properties of a medicament. Examples are: a change in an excipient (or its elimination, in the case of a dye, for instance) shown to be responsible for an adverse reaction; a change in composition (e.g., lower strength of a tablet); a change in a delivery system (e.g., from capsule to tablet to avert oesophageal insult); a change in particle size or crystalline form to overcome bioavailability or drug-delivery problems that influence unfavourably the benefit-risk balance. Child-proof packaging may also be a means of reducing the likelihood of safety problems.

5. Suspension of product licence or investigational-status approval

"Temporary suspension" of a marketed product is an option in many European countries. It is considered when the magnitude of a safety problem is still to be fully determined. The suspension may be short-term or long-term, and when the safety problem is resolved the manufacturer may resume marketing without having to submit another new-drug-application dossier.

While products are still under investigation (pre-approval), most European countries and the USA can opt to suspend clinical trials ("clinical hold") and can make the suspension permanent. "Clinical hold" gives the manufacturer and the regulatory agency time to gather more information and to review the safety issue in detail before additional patients are exposed to the product.

A related option is the suspension of reviews and decisions on marketing-application dossiers. In the case of felbamate, for example, all registration procedures in the European Union were "frozen" in July 1994 after the first reports of aplastic anaemia.

6. Withdrawal of the product from the market

Although withdrawal is probably the least desirable option for either the regulatory agency or the manufacturer, it must be considered when it becomes clear that a product's safety risks outweigh its benefits. In the instance of quinine, a thorough review showed the weakness of the efficacy data and the substantial risk of severe adverse reactions.

Occasionally, it is necessary to consider and exercise the withdrawal option even when the benefit-risk balance has not been clarified, and when specific measures for reducing risk have not been identified. The dipyrone instance illustrates this. Dipyrone was withdrawn from the market in the USA and Sweden after reports of fatal agranulocytosis. Further epidemiological study showed that the excess risk of death from this reaction was 0.10 per million dipyrone users a week. The addition of anaphylaxis, aplastic anaemia and gastrointestinal bleeding brought the total risk of death to 0.11 per million users a week, compared with 1.66 for aspirin and 1.50 for diclofenac. Years later, after resubmission of a new-drug application containing data from new studies, the drug was re-approved for marketing in Sweden.

Another example is clozapine, which was also withdrawn from some markets after reports of agranulocytosis in Finland. It was subsequently re-approved after submission of new data, with a restricted indication for schizophrenia refractory to other therapy; in addition, mandatory white-blood-cell monitoring of patients is required wherever the drug is marketed.

In the most extreme instance of product withdrawal, the regulator may judge that the newly identified risk is an "imminent hazard" to patients under treatment or who might receive the drug. The regulator should then carefully consider alerting professionals and the public and doing an immediate recall, on the basis of the following suggested criteria and questions:

How severe would be the harm that the drug might cause pending the completion of a customary review and procedure for its withdrawal or restriction?

How likely is the drug to cause such harm to users during a less immediate administrative process?

What risk would immediate withdrawal pose to current users, given the availability of other therapies and the need for patients to adjust to them?

Are there other approaches to protecting the public health?

What is the best judgment, given the information available at the time, of the likelihood that the drug will be withdrawn on the completion of the more customary administrative process?

Product withdrawal, whether voluntary by the manufacturer or mandated, necessitates consideration of a product recall to health-care professionals and patients on a regional or global basis.

7. After the analysis: Communication of new or reinforced information to the medical profession or the public

Critical to the protection of the public health is the duty to inform concerned parties when a new safety risk arises or there has been a significant change in the benefit-risk balance of a product. There are several ways of doing so, once decisions on action are made. They include changes in the wording of the standard safety sections of prescribing information or patient information leaflets, the addition of recommendations on the treatment of adverse reactions, and restriction of indications. New information might also include reinforcement on the appropriate use of a product, on dosage reduction schedules, on use of alternative therapies, or on the appropriate patient population, or "how to" instructions on product administration. The best methods of disseminating the information and the best audience for its receipt should also be carefully considered. Methods include: "dear doctor/health-professional" letters, the use of patient leaflets and advertising campaigns to health professionals or consumers, journal publications (scientific or lay press), and educational programmes/ educational materials for health professionals or consumers via print, video, audio or computer (electronic) media.

This important step in the overall process is covered in more detail in Chapter III: Decision-making.

III. DECISION-MAKING

Introduction

After the technical aspects of evaluation and their limitations have been addressed, one or more of the various options enumerated and analysed must be selected and implemented. The Working Group believes in regard to the selection of options that some fundamental concepts underlie good decision-making practices. As in most critical public health situations, decisions must be made on the basis of available evidence, tempered by prior experience, political context and professional judgment - i.e., decision-making in the face of degrees of uncertainty.

A central concept applied in such judgments is "acceptable risk" — the level of risk a population or group is prepared to accept in exchange for perceived benefits. Likewise, decision-making will be influenced by the level of "acceptable uncertainty," namely the extent to which the case for an unfavourable shift in the benefit-risk balance has been proven. As a general premise, the less society is willing to accept risk in any given situation (e.g., a product used for prophylaxis in otherwise healthy people), the less certainty decision-makers will require before they act on a new signal representing a major safety hazard. The fundamental question of "acceptable to whom," which entails the study of risk perception and risk toleration, remains a subject for continued research. For this discussion, however, the manufacturer (responsible for making medications available to people who will experience their associated benefits and risks) and regulators (responsible for protecting and advancing the health of the public) act on behalf of the target populations, who may be considered to have consented implicitly to such decision-making.

The Group observed that though details on decisions had been set out in formal legislation and regulations, little was known of the actual processes brought to bear in making these decisions. A small survey of the members of the Group and selected outside companies concerning some of their decision-making practices revealed a broad range of approaches (or none) to the seeking and harnessing of professional expertise. It included the use of public and private forums; the development and application of explicit criteria; views about the involvement of stakeholders; public meetings and proceedings; and transparency of the process and rationale of the decisions made. The main results are presented below; for details see Appendix F.

The survey findings indicated a need to establish standards in benefit-risk decision-making. Several basic concepts are described below. It is suggested that by adopting the principles outlined in the next section decision-makers will be in a position to learn progressively to improve decision-making practices and their consequences.

Basic approaches to good decision-making practices

Decision-making means determining the actions to be taken, who should take them, and the order and methods of taking action; it also entails decisions on the best means of monitoring and follow-up, and of communicating the appropriate information to the parties concerned.

It is suggested that decision-making should follow three principles: objectivity, equity and accountability.

Objectivity

Fundamental to all regulatory processes is that they must rise above impassioned arguments and partisanship and create a context in which decisions are based on the data available and are made without bias. The Working Group recognizes that precipitous decisions and actions may be taken sometimes in the face of urgent external pressures (e.g., legal, media-generated, consumer-driven), even when there is no clear and imminent hazard. Under such circumstances, however, attempts should be made to generate support for scientifically-based, adequately informed decision-making, which can assure the public that it is being well served.

Objectivity relies on several attributes or qualities of people and processes:

The evidence base: This report contains suggestions on methods of representation, array and analysis of data. As far as possible, information obtained from *all* relevant sources and by a variety of methods — observational, epidemiological and experimental — should be gathered and analysed and factored into the decision.

Expertise: The best minds available from all relevant sectors must be brought to bear on these public-health decisions.

> *The regulator:* The survey showed that all regulators used publicly established and recognized committees for this purpose, and that the committees are consistently composed of leading scholars and academics in the field. The use of ad hoc technical consultants who bring special expertise to the committee on an individual decision, as the survey indicated, is to be commended.

The manufacturer: In general, the sponsor of a drug that presents an apparent change in the benefit-risk balance undertakes an analysis independently, before or at the same time as the regulator. For this purpose, only three of the 11 surveyed companies had a standing external board to advise on benefit-risk issues; however, all reported the use of external consultants to assist in difficult situations.

The consumer: The manufacturer and the regulator, with their professional experts and advisors, must act on behalf of the population and individual patients. Some countries are exploring ways in which patients, consumers or consumer advocates can take part directly in decision-making (in our survey, only the United States regulator indicated that consumers or consumer advocates were included on some of its expert advisory panels). The Group understood the difficulty in achieving a balance between, on the one hand, public understanding and early representation of consumers in decision-making and, on the other, the risk of raising false alarms and confusing the public about difficult scientific and medical issues. In this regard, there is need of means of guarding against premature or excessive public reaction.

Avoidance of bias and conflict of interest: Because often eminent experts have been associated with the discovery and development of new medicines or are associated with direct market competitors, reviewers and referees must declare any relationships with the sponsors or their competitors which might compromise their ability to render an objective judgment. Such conflicts of interest must be revealed on all relevant occasions and discussed openly. If bias is probable, an expert may be asked to testify but not to make a recommendation or to vote.

"Scientific" decision-making: None of the participant regulators uses computer-assisted algorithms to support regulatory decisions. They are used in other areas of public policy, however, and when used appropriately have the distinct advantage that they can render explicit otherwise implicit or arbitrary assumptions and weightings of data. The Working Group recommends that consideration be given to the use of these powerful decision tools in this area.

Explicit predetermined criteria: When a drug is inherently more efficacious than others in its class, it would seem logical that it should be permitted to bear greater toxicity. But are there qualitative or quantitative criteria for how much better a drug should be to permit acceptance of higher toxicity? Or how much more toxic may it be and still have an "acceptable" benefit-risk balance? Before tackling a specific situation, it may be helpful to discuss the matter theoretically and attempt to establish bounds of acceptability — namely "criteria" against which a drug must perform. The survey of participants revealed no development or use of such explicit criteria, and the Working Group knew of no such pre-established criteria in general use in pharmaceutical decision-making. However, they are used for comparable benefit-risk purposes — in relation to environmental contamination, for instance — and their possible applicability should be explored.

Equity

A corollary of objectivity, equity demands that all drugs and other therapeutic interventions be treated fairly by ensuring comparability in requirements for evidence, analytical approaches, professional expertise and decision-making rules. These standards can be described in the following terms.

Choice of comparator: In assuring equity, there must be evidence that the benchmark product or intervention is in general use in the circumstances in which the new benefit-risk balance will prevail. Often, however, these comparator products have been on the market for many years and were approved under standards less rigorous than today's. The complete data that would allow direct comparisons may not be available, therefore. Nevertheless, every effort should be made to use the available evidence to render the best comparisons possible.

Open process: Equity requires that the major stakeholders, at least the manufacturer/sponsor, take part in regulatory decision-making. All surveyed companies reported that the regulatory authority had consulted them and that they discussed benefit-risk matters with the regulator. The survey summarized the extent to which companies participated in the most recent major safety issue handled by the regulators:

– submitted a written report   7/7 responding

– consulted for testimony   5/9

– took part directly in hearing or meeting   5/9

– took part in the discussion   4/6

Replication/consultation: Though not included in the regulatory survey, the question of interagency coordination was raised in each of the specific illustrative cases reviewed by the Working Group (Appendix B). In none did different regulators considering the issues in parallel engage in full, open, coordinated dialogue. Neither was it usual for them to review or use another agency's summary of evidence and conclusions (with the exception of review by the European Agency for the Evaluation of Medicinal Products (EMEA) of data from individual Member States). While the need for independence is understandable and different national circumstances may call for different considerations, better cross-national communication is strongly recommended.

Due process: Our survey showed that all regulatory authorities have a provision for manufacturers to appeal against a decision. In the European Union the formal appeal process ordinarily applies in all Member States. Such appeals can necessitate multiple steps through the approving agency and often adjudication by an independent commission or even the courts. In other words, other appointed representatives of society at large may eventually determine "acceptability."

Specificity: No two drugs are identical; no two benefit-risk profiles will match exactly; no two institutional or health-care environmental settings are the same. Decision-making must be specific to the circumstances. Therefore, in scientific, evidence-based decision-making, the criteria applied and the relative "weights" with which they are brought to bear on the decision must be specified. It is particularly important to indicate why one or another criterion might not be relevant to a specific benefit-risk decision.

Sensitivity: All societal benefit-risk decisions are by their very nature made in the face of uncertainty. Often this uncertainty can be expressed as confidence intervals around point estimates for specific parameters, but a certain degree of subjectivity may be needed. Given these ambiguities, the assumptions underlying the decision need to be tested. What if we are wrong? How important is it considered to be right for each of the parameters? Would a wrong assessment of a single parameter change the decision? In other words what is the level of uncertainty and does it exceed the "acceptable uncertainty" for decisions in this group of drugs or risks? If the uncertainty is too great, additional data may be required before a meaningful decision can be reached.

The extent to which society at large will come to appreciate the limitations of science and technology in benefit-risk decision-making is crucial to its acceptance of decisions made in the face of inevitable uncertainty.

Transparency: The process of decision-making, the participants and stakeholders concerned, the content of their arguments, the criteria applied to the decision, the results of sensitivity analyses — all need to be expressed in a way that will enable others to consider the applicability of the decision in different settings. This becomes especially important in collaborative circumstances (e.g., the European Union) in which decisions of an individual member state affect materially all the other states.

It is very difficult to translate these issues into a framework for public understanding in controversial or emotional circumstances, particularly when there is considerable media interest. CIOMS Working Group IV envisages a time when decision-makers will be able to present their findings and the extent of uncertainty to the public. In so doing, they will overcome the expectation of complete knowledge and certainty, which does a disservice to all parties concerned.

Accountability

Decisions are made at a specific time on the basis of the data then available. Circumstances change, however, and the effects of actions taken are rarely completely predictable. Therefore, expected outcomes (including the behaviour of health-care professionals and patients, as well as public-health impact) must be specified or estimated. In addition, as part of decision-making, criteria should be established for determining and assessing the effectiveness of the actions chosen. A recent example of such an examination is the measurement of physician compliance with changes mandated in the use of terfenadine with contraindicated concomitant drugs.[1]

After an action other than complete withdrawal of a drug, data must continue to be collected as part of the ongoing monitoring of safety. Manufacturers and regulators have generally relied for this purpose on

---

[1] Burkhart, G.A., Sevka, M.J., Temple, R. and Honig, P.K. Temporal decline in filling prescriptions for Terfenadine closely in time with those for either Ketoconazole or Erythromycin. *Clinical Pharmacology and Therapeutics,* 61: 93-96, 1997.

Thompson, D. and Oster, G. Use of Terfenadine and contraindicated drugs, *JAMA,* 275: 1339-1341, 1996.

passive collection of data, mainly spontaneous reports. However, active surveillance or a survey may be a better way to generate data to test for the expected outcomes. The data should be periodically analysed to determine whether (1) the outcomes are those desired, (2) new information dictates further review and a possible modification of the original action, or (3) there are sufficient data to consider undertaking a new benefit-risk assessment.

One country surveyed (Canada) reported a "decisional impact analysis" in which the broad range of expected consequences of regulatory actions must be stated as part of the final decision.

IV. UNADDRESSED
AND UNRESOLVED ISSUES

Owing to the complexity of an overall benefit-risk assessment, several issues remain unresolved, although they were brought to the Group's attention. Some were outside the Group's objectives and may serve as new topics for CIOMS or other groups, while others involve geographical or regional cultural or medical practice issues.

Issues outside the scope of the report

Although it was recognized that pharmaco-economic data may be important in weighing benefits and risks, economic impact was not discussed. The Group believes that economic considerations *per se* should not influence the benefit-risk assessments covered in this report. Likewise, it did not consider the ultimate economic consequences of a benefit-risk assessment and any subsequent action. Risk and benefit evaluation was considered from the perspective of patients' medical needs. Pending the full development and validation of methods of assessing therapeutic costs, the cost of treating adverse events, loss of quality of life, and other outcome-related variables, the use of such methods is considered premature.

The Group did not address in any detail impact analysis of the decision options available after conducting a benefit-risk assessment. Also beyond its objectives were methods of assessing the success of communication and other action initiated with professionals and patients, and their subsequent behaviour.

Benefit-risk assessment and decision-making can be subject to strong cultural and ethnic influences; different countries or populations may weigh differently the same evidence for benefits and risks. This applies especially to the definition or perception of "acceptable" risk.

Once regulatory/manufacturer decisions are made on the basis of a benefit-risk assessment, the results must be communicated to the parties concerned. Although this report suggests points to consider for this activity, it was beyond the scope of the project to develop specific recommendations on how, to whom, by whom and when such communication should be directed. The Group recognizes the need for improvement and guidelines in this area, and a separate CIOMS initiative is dealing with some of these issues.

Formal decision-making theory has been increasingly applied to the practice of medicine[1], but the Working Group did not consider elaboration of its techniques and their application to benefit-risk evaluation.

Unresolved issues

How severe or serious or frequent should a risk be to trigger a benefit-risk re-assessment? There are quantitative approaches for determining whether a number of case-reports exceeds background risk[2], and judgment is always required, but more-systematic approaches would be valuable.

Some believe that a metric is needed that would combine severity and incidence of reactions. How could such an index be constructed and validated?

Is it possible to establish an algorithm for benefit-risk assessment? This would require an expert system but all the values are not yet known and inferential rules are not validated.

A decision to withdraw a drug from the market may appear acceptable at the population level but individuals who might benefit from it might still opt for its use. This and other considerations affect the ethical aspects of whether benefit-risk assessments can and should be conducted for a patient, a population or a special group.

Risk perception and risk communication are central to the weighing of benefits and risks. However, it is extremely difficult to factor these into the assessment and decision-making processes described. Although assessment is made and action taken from a public-health perspective on behalf of individuals, how much risk is a patient, given a choice, willing to take for how much benefit? How relevant to everyday medical practice are very rare but medically serious adverse reactions, and how should such information be communicated to a patient? These issues need considerable research. An example of the dilemmas faced, without resolution, relates to the morbidity

---

[1] Schumaker, G.E. Multiattribute Evaluation in Formulary Decisionmaking as Applied to Calcium-channel Blockers. *American Journal of Hospital Pharmacists*, 48: 301-306, 1991.

Eriksen, S. and Keller, L. Robin. A Multiattribute-utility-function Approach to Weighing the Risks and Benefits of Pharmaceutical Agents. *Medical Decisionmaking* 13: 118-125, 1993.

Sox, H.C., Jr., Blatt, M.A. Higgins, M.C., and Manton, K.I. *Medical Decisionmaking*. Butterworth, Stoneham, Massachussets, 1988.

[2] Begaud, B., Moride, Y., Tubert-Bitter, P., Chasterie, A. and Haramburu, F. False-positives in Spontaneous Reporting: Should We Worry About Them? *British Journal of Clinical Pharmacology*, 38:401-414,1994.

Edwards, R., Lindquist, M., Wilholm, B.-E. and Napke, E. Quality Criteria for Early Signals of Possible Adverse Drug Reactions, *Lancet*, 336:156-158, 1990.

statistics associated with Stevens-Johnson syndrome and toxic epidermal necrolysis as they affect the choice of various therapeutic options.[3]

By influencing public opinion, lay and scientific media often influence considerably a government or a company's opportunity to make rational, scientifically-based decisions. Ideally, health professionals should be informed before decisions and information are communicated to the public. However, a dialogue with the media is needed on these issues, which often have ethical implications.

The elaboration of the many inadequately defined or poorly studied parameters affecting benefit-risk analysis or of the factors that influence it would be very beneficial. Among the more obvious are better measures of exposure of patients to drugs and of patient compliance as well as better use of the resulting data, the extent and impact of off-label use or misuse of medicines, dose-effect relationships (for desired and undesired effects), background/natural-history data for signal events in at-risk populations, and mechanisms of drug-induced diseases. Their elaboration might lead to means of identifying patient-groups or particular patients predisposed to serious adverse reactions.

[3] Roujeau, J.-C., Kelly, J. P., Naldi, L. et al. Medication Use and the Risk of Stevens-Johnson syndrome or toxic epidermal necrolysis, *New England Journal of Medicine*, 333:1600-1607, 1995 and 334:922-923, 1996.

V. OVERALL SUMMARY
OF PROPOSALS

The key ideas and proposals of the CIOMS Working Group are presented in succinct form as "take-away messages", in the order in which the subjects were discussed in Chapters I through IV,

General Principles

The approach proposed is intended to be applicable only in the case of a suspected major safety problem.

Typically, signals arise from market experience, but information from all sources must be used in benefit-risk assessment.

The CIOMS IV approach addresses the population at risk, not the patient at risk.

If crisis-management techniques are needed, a thorough benefit-risk assessment is still necessary.

Although, typically, a benefit-risk assessment is prompted by a new, important risk, the impact of the new signal must be reviewed in the total context of the profile and use of the drug.

Problems may be intrinsically related to active ingredients, metabolites or excipients of products, and these are to be distinguished from accidental or intentional contamination or defects.

Although economic considerations increasingly affect health-care systems, they should not influence the types of benefit-risk assessment covered here. Nevertheless, willingness to accept risk may depend on cost in many parts of the world, where authorities may need to consider expense in their decision-making.

As much cooperation and exchange of needed information as possible should take place as promptly as possible between the parties concerned, usually companies and regulators.

The need for urgent action to protect the public must be weighed against the need for additional data that might provide better conclusions.

Although the main thrust of this report is to provide guidance to manufacturers and regulators, the affected parties should be engaged in the decision process when possible.

Introduction to a Report

Briefly introduce the drug so that the report "stands alone" and will not be misinterpreted.

Where and for how long has the drug been marketed? What are its indications by country?

Are data from co-marketers or licensees included?

Alternative therapies or modalities, including surgery, should be indicated at this stage, along with the reasons for the manufacturer's choice. Ideally, fair comparison will require the same indications and duration of treatment for the alternatives. Also an effort should be made to match the severity of the disease treated, concomitant medications, and age and sex distribution of the affected populations.

Benefit Evaluation

(A more extensive check-list of points to consider in evaluating benefits is found at the end of Chapter II B.)

A benefit-risk analysis should begin with a discussion of a drug's benefits.

First, the epidemiology and natural history of the target disease should be described:

What is its incidence/prevalence?

Are there high-risk populations?

Is the disease self-limiting, fatal or disabling; does it have considerable morbidity; or is the condition being treated an asymptomatic risk-factor for subsequent disease?

If the disease is the direct target of treatment, what is its associated morbidity and mortality?

Comparative benefit-risk evaluation of a drug can be highly situational; it varies according to its intended application and the circumstances in which it is to be used, such as:

- prevention or treatment?
- life-threatening or self-limiting disease?
- to prevent disease progression or to cure?

- to treat chronic disabling symptoms or to reduce or delay morbidity/mortality?
- as an orphan drug in a limited population with no therapeutic alternative?
- occurrence of adverse reactions with unapproved use?
- therapeutic response different in sub-populations?
- first-line or second-line therapy?

Benefit may be defined with regard to the individual or to society (e.g., the net benefit of a vaccine to society).

What is the drug's absolute efficacy, viz., the number of deaths prevented or patients cured for symptomatic treatment? Over what length of time and in what percentage of patients is the drug effective?

If it is designed to prevent disease, to what extent is the disease risk-factor affected and what is the associated reduction of disease risk?

Where surrogate measurements are used, what is the evidence that they are valid markers?

Take into account the extent to which benefits have been demonstrated and the quality of the data.

Are there any negative studies? Is the supportive scientific literature of high quality? Have such measurements as quality-adjusted-life-years been validated?

What is the degree of benefit achieved in relation to alternative therapies or interventions and their relative efficacy and effectiveness?

Even if there is alternative therapy, what is the effect of no treatment?

As tolerability is likely to affect compliance, the comparison of the drug with alternatives should also be discussed, with regard to route of administration, frequency of dosing, palatability and other factors related to convenience.

Risk Evaluation

Introduction

Unlike the benefits of a drug, which are usually distinct or well-defined, risks usually comprise a mixture of adverse reactions.

The medical impact of an adverse reaction is characterized by its frequency of occurrence, duration and intensity, and different reactions are not directly comparable unless they can be expressed by a common measure.

Formal analysis of absolute and relative risks is never made with total knowledge.

General considerations in an analysis

Begin with a history of how the new issue was identified.

Provide a thorough review of the evidence associated with the new safety issue, including temporal relationship, physicochemical characteristics, possibility of a class effect, possible role of interactions, background incidence of the event, and the possibility of a subgroup at risk.

Discuss the strength of the evidence (as described in detail in the report of CIOMS Working Group III).

Address the preventability, predictability and reversibility of the reaction.

The adverse reaction that dominates the overall risk profile (carries the most weight) is referred to as the *risk driver* or *dominant risk*.

In addition to data on the signal adverse reaction, all other adverse-reaction data on the product should be considered in describing and quantifying the overall risk; this applies especially to other serious or frequent reactions.

Typically, a single medicinal product is evaluated for risk without reference to its alternative therapies, but comparative risk assessments, which are crucial and more relevant, are more difficult, for many reasons.

For comparators, three key elements, namely qualitative descriptions of the relevant adverse reactions (including their duration), their frequency, and a weighting of relative importance ("seriousness"), should optimally provide an opportunity for numerical comparison.

As a first step, the three most often reported and the three most serious adverse reactions can be chosen as representatives for the risk profile of each medicine in the comparison.

For risk weighing for individual adverse reactions, there is no obvious metric or methodology.

What methods are available? Some companies have lists of medically serious conditions; the WHO Collaborating Centre for International Drug Monitoring uses a "critical terms" list.

Agreed scales or values for adverse reactions would contribute to standardization; the issue is an important area for research.

The Working Group suggests the use of standard visual presentations, usually as bar graphs, to represent risk profiles of individual drugs, classified by subgroup (e.g., serious, fatal, or other adverse-reaction categories). Units, periods of time covered and other key elements integral to interpretation should be clearly indicated on any form of presentation.

To avoid combining data inappropriately, separate profiles should be established for data from different sources, such as spontaneous reports and clinical trials.

In the absence of comprehensive information, other data sources might include official data-sheets or data from regulatory registries (e.g., from the United States Food and Drug Administration through the Freedom of Information mechanism or from the ADROIT data-base of the United Kingdom Medicines Control Agency).

Different populations, indications and dosage forms may also necessitate separate risk profiles.

Quantification of risk: To put the newly identified risk into perspective, it should be quantified in terms of incidence, but this is usually difficult to do precisely.

Excess incidence of reaction ("drug attributable incidence") is a more meaningful measure. Calculation of within-drug excess incidence from comparative clinical trials or cohort observational studies is straightforward, but case/control studies are somewhat more complicated.

It is more difficult to compare various alternative drugs for incidence of adverse reactions, in part because of their usually different marketing histories.

The distinction between "absolute" and "relative" risk must be kept in mind. The significance of a high relative risk (e.g.,1.5) depends considerably on whether the actual incidence of an event is 1 in 10 or 1 in 100,000.

Estimated total drug risk: Once standard units are selected as markers for comparison, the weighted excess incidence rate can be calculated for each adverse reaction by multiplying the excess incidence rate by the weight factor specific to the adverse reaction.

To obtain the weighted overall excess incidence of the combined reactions of interest, the sum of the individual values provides an aggregate (e.g., for the three most serious reactions).

To obtain the incremental drug-attributable risk, the aggregate values must be subtracted from a reference standard treatment (or no treatment).

Validity of the estimates: To test the robustness of the risk estimation, sensitivity analyses can be performed. Great care must also be taken in any attempt to extrapolate beyond the specific populations; if total risk estimates are extrapolated all assumptions must be stated.

Suggested sequential overall approach: The Working Group suggests a 12-step, general methodological approach to risk assessment.

Benefit-Risk Evaluation

Comparison of benefits and risks, even of a single product, is a deceptively simple concept; comparison of the trade-offs between benefits and risks among various products is particularly difficult.

One problem is that benefits and risks are usually expressed in different parameters and units. Some simple attempts have been made to combine benefits and risks, such as:

- global assessment made by a treating physician to reflect a patient's overall response to treatment
- a benefit-risk ratio, defined as the number of efficacy events needed for each occurrence of a serious adverse event
- an "incremental benefit-risk ratio," i.e., the number of additional cases of severe toxicity for each therapeutic success.

In addition to efficacy (morbidity under "ideal" conditions) and effectiveness (under ordinary conditions) other measures might include quality of life, quantity of life and cost efficiency. However, more research is needed to test their validity for use in comparative benefit-risk assessment.

Certain basic principles apply in benefit-risk assessment:

All available relevant data on benefits and risks should be assembled

Be transparent in the way data are presented

Comparable outcome measures should be used for comparison

Explore whether it is possible to determine whether a specific subgroup is at particular risk

Adverse reactions are characterized by their:

- seriousness
- duration
- incidence

Benefits can be assessed in terms of the effects of the drug on the target disease as regards its:

- seriousness
- chronicity
- extent of control of the target disease

The incidence metric for adverse reactions does not apply to benefits except for prophylaxis or vaccination (what is the incidence of the disease with and without the preventive agent?).

Among different approaches recommended, use the above descriptors to express benefits and risks associated with each product, focusing on the three most serious and three most common reactions, including the signal-generating event.

Judgment is needed in any categorization rubric of benefits and risks (e.g., categorization by levels of seriousness, duration, incidence); the conceptual framework for such a scheme may be used as a simple algorithm to maintain a consistent logic.

It may be possible to represent benefits and risks quantitatively and graphically.

Use of the expression "benefit-risk ratio" or any single "overall" expression of risk or benefit is discouraged.

It is emphasized that the approaches discussed involve a consistent logic but cannot always serve as standard methodologies. There is no consensus on a single method; indeed different approaches are likely to be needed for individual situations.

The results should always be framed in the proper therapeutic context and presented in terms of both relative and absolute expressions of benefit and risk.

Options Analysis

Among the options for action available to regulators and manufacturers are the following:

- maintaining the status quo

- "watching and waiting" (i.e., monitoring subsequent experience)
- additional data-gathering/initiation of new research (clinical or non-clinical)
- modification of product information, distribution or manufacture
- restriction of product availability
- suspension of product licence
- withdrawal of the product from the market

Whenever possible, the advantages and disadvantages (pros and cons) of each option should be described in the context of the specific situation. Also include an impact analysis which outlines the anticipated consequences.

Central to the interests of all, whichever the chosen option, is the need for clear and effective communication.

Decision-Making

Decisions must be made on the basis of the available evidence, tempered by prior experience, political context and professional judgment.

A central concept is "acceptable risk," but the fundamental question is: "acceptable to whom."

In decision-making there should be three broad principles: objectivity, equity and accountability.

Objectivity relies on:
- the evidence base
- expertise
- the regulator
- the manufacturer
- the consumer
- avoidance of bias and conflict of interest

Equity demands comparability in terms of:
- choice of comparator
- open process (involvement of all relevant parties)
- replication/consultation (e.g., interregulatory dialogue)
- due process (a provision to appeal a decision)

- specificity to the circumstances
- sensitivity (i.e., what is the level of uncertainty)
- transparency (i.e., the results expressed in a way which will enable others to understand the rationale of the decision).

Accountability requires that expected outcomes are defined and criteria specified for assessing the effectiveness in practice of the option chosen.

Following an action other than complete drug withdrawal, collection of data must be continued in order to monitor the expected outcomes.

Work is encouraged on development of more powerful decision tools and better measurement criteria for a medicine's performance.

Unaddressed and Unresolved Issues

Issues outside the scope of the report

Economic considerations *per se*

Impact analysis of the decision

Benefit-risk evaluations and decision-making in relation to cultural and ethnic influences

Specific recommendations on how, to whom, by whom and when communication on the results and decisions should be directed

Decision-making theory and its application to benefit-risk evaluations.

Unresolved issues

How substantial must a risk be to trigger a benefit-risk assessment?

A metric combining severity and incidence of adverse reactions

An algorithm for conducting benefit-risk assessment

The ethical aspects of whether benefit-risk assessments can and should be conducted for a patient, a population or a special group

Risk-perception and risk-communication: how best to factor these elements into the assessment and decision-making processes

Dialogue with the media on their role, which often raises ethical considerations

Finally, the elaboration of many influences and parameters would be beneficial: e.g., better measures of patient exposure and patient compliance and better use of the data, the extent of off-label use or misuse of medicines, and data on the natural history (background incidence) of signal events in the populations at risk.

VI. GLOSSARY

Key terms are defined or described here. Most have no universally accepted definitions, though some regulatory authorities have adopted "official" definitions for some. Consequently, the definitions and descriptions are annotated with explanations to ensure that the meanings provided are understood with regard to their use in the context of this report. Whenever possible, literature or other citations are given for previously established definitions. The absence of inverted commas for referenced definitions indicates that they were paraphrased for use in the present report.

Benefit: Benefit usually refers to a gain (positive result) for an individual or a population. "Expected" benefit can be expressed quantitatively, and this would ordinarily incorporate an estimate of the probability of achieving the gain.

These uses of the term *benefit* are those employed in this report.

Some current definitions of *benefit* include reference not only to clinical improvement but also to quality of life and economic consequences, as in the following example:[1]

"The improvement attributable to the drug, in terms of human health, health-related quality of life, and/or economic benefit to the individual or group."

This definition is beyond the scope of the concepts developed in this CIOMS report.

Dominant risk: The risk that is considered to be the major contributor to the overall risk profile.

Note: Other terms used to describe the dominant risk are, e.g., *primary risk* or *risk driver*. Dominant risk is the one adverse reaction that outweighs the others in the overall risk profile and risk management of the product.

Efficacy: Efficacy is the ability of a medicine or medical technology to bring about the intended beneficial effect on individuals in a defined population with a given medical problem, under ideal conditions of use.

Note: Efficacy generally refers to how well a particular medicine will bring about the intended effect under "ideal" or near ideal conditions, as in a clinical-trial setting, for example.

---

[1] *Benefit, Risk and Cost Management of Drugs.* Report of the CPHA National Advisory Panel on Risk/Benefit Management of Drugs. Canadian Public Health Association, January 1993.

Effectiveness: Effectiveness is a measure of the effect a medicine (or medical technology) is purported, or is represented, to have under conditions for the use prescribed, recommended or labelled.

> **Note:** Effectiveness refers to how well a drug achieves its intended effect in the usual clinical setting ("real world") and reflects its impact in the community (benefits observed at the population level).[2]

Hazard: A situation that under particular circumstances could lead to harm. A source of danger.

Relative risk: The ratio of the incidence rate of an outcome (event) in an exposed group to the incidence rate of the outcome (event) in an unexposed group.[3]

Risk: The simple, standard, epidemiological definition of risk is *the probability that something will happen.*

> **Note:** In the context of medical interventions (drugs, e.g.), the "something" is almost always associated with a negative event. In defining or describing a specific risk, it is always important to include information on intensity (severity, e.g.), time of the event (onset or duration), and time period over which the probability applies. Some definitions attempt to include concepts of rate, intensity and time:
>
> *The probability of the occurrence of an adverse or untoward outcome and the severity of the resultant harm to the health of individuals in a defined population, associated with the use of a medical technology for a specified medical problem under specified conditions of use.*

Risk evaluation: Risk evaluation is the complex process of determining the significance or value of the identified hazards and estimated risks to those concerned with or affected by the process.

Risk management: The making of decisions concerning risks, or action to reduce the consequences or probability of occurrence.[4]

Serious: Usually the word "serious" has two connotations. One is the common use of the term "medically serious," implying a diagnosis or condition that is dangerous, critical or alarming. The other is a regulatory-administrative definition created for purposes of defining regulatory reporting obligations for adverse reaction reports. Although different regulators use several similar definitions, the following definition encompasses

---

[2] Abramson, J.H., *Survey Methods in Community Medicine*, 4th Edition, p. 49. Churchill Livingstone, New York (1990); and Cochrane, A.L. *Effectiveness and Efficiency, Random Refections on Health Services.* Nuffield Provincial Hospital Trust, London, 1972.

[3] B.L. Strom, ed., *Pharmacoepidemiology.* John Wiley and Sons, New York, 1994.

[4] *Risk: Analysis, Perception and Management.* Report of a Royal Society Study Group. The Royal Society, London, 1992.

all of them and is the official definition given in the 1995 Guideline on expedited reporting of adverse drug reactions, of the International Conference on Harmonization of Technical Requirements for Registration of Pharmaceuticals for Human Use (ICH)[5]:

A serious adverse event (experience) or reaction is any untoward medical occurrence that at any dose:

- *results in death*
- *is life-threatening*
- *requires inpatient hospitalization or prolongation of hospitalization*
- *results in persistent or significant disability/incapacity*
- *is a congenital anomaly/birth defect.*

Medical and scientific judgement should be exercised in deciding whether expedited reporting is appropriate in other situations, such as important medical events that may not be immediately life-threatening or result in death or hospitalization but may jeopardize the patient or may require intervention to prevent one of the other outcomes listed in the definition above. These should also usually be considered serious.

Severe/Severity: The term *severe* is not synonymous with *serious* in this context. *Severe* is used to describe the intensity (severity) of a specific event (as in mild, moderate or severe myocardial infarction).

Signal: A report (or reports) of an event that may have a causal relationship to one or more drugs; it alerts health professionals and should be explored further.[6]

Note: In addition to information on a new (unexpected), potentially important event, a signal can refer to an unexpected finding, or a finding exceeding a determined threshold, for an already known event — for example, data involving the nature (specificity), intensity or rate of occurrence.

[5] Gordon, A.J. *Implementation and Impact of ICH Guideline E2A: Definitions and Standards for Expedited Reporting.* Proceedings of the Third International Conference on Harmonization, Queens University, Belfast, pp. 461-469, 1996.

[6] Hartzema, A.G., Porta, M.S. and Tilson, H.H. *Pharmacoepidemiology: An Introduction.* Harvey, Whitney Books. Cincinnati, Ohio, 1988.

APPENDIX A

MEMBERSHIP AND ACTIVITIES
OF CIOMS WORKING GROUP IV

The Working Group was composed of representatives of five European and four United States pharmaceutical companies; of the European Agency for the Evaluation of Medicinal Products (EMEA) and of regulatory authorities in Canada, Denmark, France, Germany, Italy, Japan, Sweden, the United Kingdom, and the United States of America; of the World Health Organization (WHO) (Geneva) and the WHO Collaborating Centre for International Drug Monitoring (Uppsala, Sweden), and, as observers, of the EMEA and the Bundesverband der Pharmazeutischen Industrie (BPI, Germany). There were also three independent consultants and one invited expert. The Group met six times between January 1995 and October 1996; sub-groups met at various times through the end of 1997.

1. London January 1995	The Group outlined the scope of the task and explored concepts.
2. Boston June 1995	Concepts were refined and the report chapters were defined. Small sub-groups were allocated individual chapters. Twenty-four members independently scored 20 different adverse-reaction terms selected arbitrarily by Win Castle.
3. Frankfurt October 1995	The first drafts of each chapter were discussed. Additional assignments were designated, mainly related to gathering and summarizing data on the drug case-histories chosen as illustrative examples. Fourteen members repeated the earlier survey exercise without access to their earlier assessments to determine whether the results were reproducible.
4. London February 1996	The case histories were presented and agreed. Hugh Tilson and Sue Roden presented the results of their survey on how regulators and manufacturers made decisions for action on benefit-risk reviews.

5. Copenhagen May 1996	Each chapter was reviewed, and Win Castle and Arnold Gordon undertook to prepare the first draft of the report.
6. Philadelphia October 1996	The first draft was reviewed and amendments, corrections and additional modifications were suggested.
7. Philadelphia, April 1997 and Geneva, July 1997	Review of draft 2 led to more changes. Arnold Gordon prepared another draft, which Win Castle and Mac Lumpkin reviewed; after final changes and corrections the manuscript was submitted to CIOMS in February 1998 for publication.

The full-time members of the Working Group and their affiliations at the time were:

Zbigniew Bankowski	– CIOMS (Geneva)
Christian Bénichou	– Synthélabo (Paris)
Annekarin Bertelsmann	– EMEA
Rudolf Bruppacher	– Ciba-Geigy and as independent consultant (Basel)
Win Castle	– Independent consultant (Raleigh, North Carolina) and SmithKline Beecham (US) (Co-Chair)
Anne Castot	– Agence du Médicament (Saint-Denis, France)
Diane Chen	– Independent consultant (Gloucester, Massachusetts)
Gaby Danan	– Roussel Uclaf (Paris)
Ralph Edwards	– WHO Collaborating Centre for International Drug Monitoring (Uppsala, Sweden)
Arnold Gordon	– Pfizer (New York) (Editor in Chief)
Gottfried Kreutz	– Bundesinstitut für Arzneimittel und Medizinprodukte (Berlin)
Mac Lumpkin	– Food and Drug Administration (Rockville, Maryland, USA) (Co-Chair)

Carlos Martinez	– HMR (Frankfurt am Main)
Danielle Muzard	– Eli Lilly (Saint Cloud, France)
Sue Roden	– Glaxo Wellcome (Greenford) (Secretary)
Bruce Rowsell	– HPB (Ontario)
Jens Schou	– University of Copenhagen and CPMP
Barbara Sickmüller	– BPI (Frankfurt am Main)
Wendy Stephenson	– Merck Research Laboratories (West Point, PA)
Ryuichi Takahashi	– Ministry of Health and Welfare (Tokyo)
Martijn ten Ham	– World Health Organization (Geneva)
Hugh Tilson	– Glaxo Wellcome (Raleigh, North Carolina)
Bengt-Erik Wiholm	– National Board of Health (Uppsala, Sweden)
Susan Wood	– Medicines Control Agency (London)

The following attended one or two meetings only:

M. Collela	– Ministry of Health (Rome)
Margaret Cone	– International Federation of Pharmaceutical Manufacturers Associations (Geneva)
Tadayumi Fukita	– Takeda Chemical Industries (Osaka)
Tatsuo Kurokawa	– Ministry of Health and Welfare (Tokyo)
George Lagier	– Pharmacologie Hôpital Fernand Widal (France)
Carmela Santuccio	– Ministry of Health (Rome)
E. Uchiyama	– Ministry of Health and Welfare (Tokyo)
Ernst Weidmann	– HMR (Frankfurt am Main)
Jean-Michel Weiss	– Hoffman-La Roche (Basel)

Dr William W. Lowrance (Geneva) provided consultation during the project.

APPENDIX B

ILLUSTRATIVE CASE HISTORIES
OF BENEFIT-RISK ASSESSMENT

The seven case histories differ in format and content, largely because of the differing amounts and types of information available on the clinical data, the regulatory review process, options for decisions considered and the decision-making process. The information was obtained from public regulatory records, publications, and non-proprietary company sources.

1. Quinine and allergic haematological events

2. Felbamate and blood dyscrasias

3. Dipyrone and agranulocytosis

4. Temafloxacin and renal impairment, and hypoglycaemia in elderly patients

5. Remoxipride and blood dyscrasias

6. Clozapine and agranulocytosis

7. Sparfloxacin and phototoxicity

1. Quinine

Background

Quinine had over-the-counter (OTC) status in the United States and was indicated for the treatment of nocturnal leg cramps. It was manufactured by a number of companies and regulated by standards set out in a tentative monograph. As it was marketed prior to 1962 it remained on the market until it could be reviewed for safety and efficacy. In the 1970s and '80s public panels were set up to examine OTC products and decide whether they should be discontinued, given full final monograph status (i.e., full data were available), or reviewed later when new data became available. Quinine was placed in this last category.

On 22 August 1994 there was a general review of the safety of quinine for OTC status because of allergic haematological events.

Quinine was available as 200 mg and 300 mg tablets.

Benefit

Data were available from only six clinical trials, sponsored by different manufacturers. The data did not support the efficacy of the product, either because the analyses were flawed, or several confounding factors were present, or there was no demonstrable difference between quinine and placebo.

Risk

Sensory disturbances and visual and auditory symptoms (symptoms of quinine toxicity) were seen in special studies in which therapeutic doses were used.

Serious hypersensitivity reactions had occurred, including thrombocytopenia. Patients had been hospitalized and some had died. There was no method of predicting and, therefore, warning about thrombocytopenia, which occurred at an incidence of between 1 in 1000 and 1 in 3500 treated patients.

Options analysis

The options available were:

- remove from the market for the indication
- restrict use
- transfer to prescription status
- restrict to compassionate use (named-patient use)

However, a drug cannot be transferred from one status to another if it is not effective. If a drug can be OTC it should be. To be a prescription medicine it would be necessary to show that the indication cannot be self-diagnosed or the drug used safely.

Decision/outcome

After February 1995, quinine was no longer recognized in the United States as safe and effective for the treatment of leg cramps, and the indication was withdrawn.

The process was transparent and the public and the profession were informed by press releases and articles in nursing and medical journals.*

---

* See Federal Register, Volume 59, No. 161, Monday, August 22, 1994. 21 CFR Part 310 *Drug Products for the Treatment and/or Prevention of Nocturnal Leg Muscle Cramps for Over-the-Counter Human Use; Final Rule.* Also see Chase, S.L. *FDA Yanks Leg Cramp Product off the OTC Market*, R.N., 58(5): 71, 1995 and Leclerc, K.M. and Landry, F.J. *Benign Nocturnal Leg Cramps.* Current Controversies Over Use of Quinine, *Postgraduate Medicine*, 99(2): 181-184, 1996.

Points illustrated

A mild, self-limiting disease treated with a drug that caused a rare, serious (sometimes fatal), and unpredictable reaction

Problems associated with old drugs: a different process is probably required as there may be no proper efficacy data

Effect of OTC status as distinct from prescription status

Consequences of decision

Risk estimation in the absence of efficacy.

2. Felbamate

Background

Felbamate is an antiepileptic drug, marketed in the United States since September 1993 and in Europe since March 1994.

The drug was first indicated as monotherapy or adjunctive therapy for partial epileptic seizures which may or may not become generalized in adults and as adjunctive therapy for partial and generalized seizures associated with Lennox-Gastaut syndrome in children. Except for one country, the European Commission through its Committee on Proprietary Medicinal Products (CPMP) (March 1994) approved the drug for monotherapy or adjunctive therapy for adults and for adolescents of over 14 years with partial onset seizures not controlled with other anti-epileptic agents. France was the rapporteur.

In June 1994 the company sent reports of five poorly documented spontaneous cases of aplastic anaemia to the different authorities. Further to other reports of blood dyscrasia (leucopenia and thrombocytopenia) occurring during a compassionate-use programme, and following three other cases of aplastic anaemia, the European Commission's Committee for Proprietary Medical Products in agreement with the French authorities decided in July 1994 to suspend all registration procedures and marketing, and recommended that haematological and clinical follow-up studies be conducted.

In August 1994, after examination of new cases of aplastic anaemia, the French authorities discontinued compassionate use and stopped inclusion of new patients in clinical trials. The US Food and Drug Administration informed the prescribers of the occurrence of aplastic anaemia and modified the package insert to include warnings, restriction of indication, and a recommendation on haematological monitoring.

From entering the market in the United States up to the beginning of October 1994, 32 cases of aplastic anaemia were reported; 16 serious hepatic disorders were also reported to the French regulatory authorities.

Based on an estimated treated population of 120,000 patients by October 1994, the incidence can be estimated as at least 1/4000 treated patients. No cases were reported during clinical trials in the development programme, in which about 1600 patients took part; there were some reports of decreased white-blood-cell counts, but none of aplastic anaemia or agranulocytosis.

The characteristics of the cases are as follows:

All the patients developed pancytopenia with severe thrombocytopenia, and in all cases the bone-marrow biopsy was consistent with aplastic anaemia; most patients presented with signs of infection or bleeding. In 37% of cases, pancytopenia was discovered during a systematic blood count. There were 21 females and 11 males of 12 to 70 years of age and one child of 21 months.

In 34% of cases the onset was sudden, with an immediate diagnosis.

The median time to onset was five months. In one case the diagnosis was made nearly six weeks after felbamate had been discontinued.

In 34% of cases felbamate was the only drug that could have been involved.

In two cases rechallenge was positive.

In all cases the outcome was serious. Nine died (28%) and four others received transplants.

The clinical-trial pattern is similar for all cases — aplastic anaemia seems to be a severe complication of treatment with felbamate and occurs after a mean duration of treatment of about 5.6 months. The occurrence is sudden, with serious thrombocytopenia that regresses very slowly. A causal relationship seems probable. All cases have the same profile. In a few cases there was no other aetiology or drug that could account for aplastic anaemia.

The benefits

Lennox-Gastaut syndrome is a dramatic, life-threatening epileptic encephalopathy, which occurs in a well-defined population, especially children. Most patients are often refractory to all antiepileptic drugs; felbamate has demonstrated its efficacy in atonic seizures. The only therapeutic alternative is surgery, and its associated risk must also be taken into account.

The risks

Aplastic anaemia is a very rare but severe disorder, with a background incidence of 1-20/1,000,000 person-years; the risk associated with felbamate is considered to be about 200 times greater than the background incidence. The prognosis is poor, with a death rate of about 25%.

It is difficult to know whether the drug-induced cases could have been prevented by blood monitoring and early discontinuation of the drug; however, regular monitoring may prevent irreversible aplastic anaemia.

Given the available data, it is impossible to determine the mechanism; the mean interval of onset is not characteristic of an immuno-allergic reaction. Thus, an idiosyncratic reaction is probable but no clear risk factors have been found.

Options considered

Complete withdrawal: Felbamate is the only drug that leads to a major improvement in the quality of life, with a dramatic decrease in the number of fits, in Lennox-Gastaut syndrome. It appears to be the last alternative treatment before surgery.

Maintenance of the marketing authorization with:

- very restrictive indications; felbamate could be kept only as second-line treatment for patients with Lennox-Gastaut syndrome or partial-onset seizures that are refractory to all available antiepileptic drugs, including the most recent

- informed consent from the patient before felbamate therapy is begun

- strict conditions for the prescription and restriction of supply (hospital use, neurologists)

- clear information on the risk of aplastic anaemia and hepatitis, and recommendations on monitoring of blood and liver (Summary of Product Characteristics (SmPC)) modifications, boxed warning, Dear Doctor letter).

Withdrawal of the marketing authorization but making the drug available to treat a small number of patients under compassionate use.

Decision-Making

The Committee for Proprietary Medical Products (CPMP)

The CPMP at its December 1994 meeting decided to keep the drug on the market because a very limited epileptic population needed it, with strict prescribing conditions and requirements for treatment surveillance.

Because of the seriousness and the frequency of aplastic anaemia reported with felbamate, but in view of the expected benefit of the drug to children resistant to other antiepileptic drugs, the indication was restricted to Lennox-Gastaut syndrome in patients aged 4 years or more and refractory to all available antiepileptic medicinal products.

The company was obliged to undertake a post-authorization surveillance study in all patients receiving felbamate. To do so, the company proposed to send a letter to all potential felbamate prescribers, and to establish a register of all treated patients (pre-paid card, to be returned to the company at the initiation or discontinuation of treatment). All potential prescribers were sent a letter setting out the risks and recommended monitoring.

The Summary of Product Characteristics (SmPC) was subsequently modified accordingly.

The Food and Drug Administration (FDA)

In the United States felbamate is restricted to patients with such severe epilepsy that the benefits of felbamate outweigh its risks (refractory epileptics who respond inadequately to other anticonvulsant drugs).

As of 1996, of 20,000 US patients originally on felbamate, 10,000 were still taking the drug after inclusion of the black box warning, restricted indications, and 26,000 Dear Doctor letters. There had been 10 cases of hepatic failure, of which four had been fatal and one had had a liver transplant.

Points illustrated

This example highlights the difficulty of a benefit-risk assessment when the disease is so severe that a very serious drug risk can be acceptable. The decision-making took into account the need for each physician to make a benefit-risk assessment for each patient.

3. Dipyrone

Background

Dipyrone is one of the non-narcotic analgesics (NNA) that have no anti-inflammatory action. It is an effective medicine for the treatment of fever and pain and is used in more than 100 countries, including Germany, France, Spain, Italy and Finland.

Dipyrone was introduced into clinical therapy in 1922 and registered in Sweden in 1934 for the treatment of various states of acute pain. Because of the risk of agranulocytosis it was withdrawn from the Swedish and US markets in 1974 and 1977, respectively. At that time, the number of spontaneous reports suggested a causal relationship between dipyrone and agranulocytosis.

To provide population-based evidence for the adverse public-health impact of dipyrone, the International Agranulocytosis and Aplastic Anaemia Study (IAAAS) was carried out in 1980-1986. It provided a more precise assessment of the occurrence of agranulocytosis and its associated mortality than earlier studies had. The re-evaluation of the clinical safety data indicated that the risk of agranulocytosis had been overestimated in the 1970s. Consequently, in 1994 Hoechst resubmitted an application for marketing approval of dipyrone in Sweden.

Benefits

In addition to its antipyretic activities dipyrone is an effective oral and parenteral treatment for moderate to severe post-operative pain. Oral dipyrone is superior to acetylsalicylic acid and comparable or superior to paracetamol. In its parenteral form it compares in analgesic efficacy to non-steroidal anti-inflammatory drug (NSAID) therapy and weak opioids.

Risks

Materials and methods

All potentially fatal adverse events (AEs) reported in connection with non-narcotic analgesics (NNAs) were identified: anaphylaxis, Stevens-Johnson syndrome and toxic epidermal necrolysis (SJS/TEN), agranulocytosis, aplastic anaemia, upper gastrointestinal complications (haemorrhage or perforation), toxic liver disease and end-stage renal failure. The Medline database was searched for all English-language reports of epidemiological studies published between January 1970 and November 1995 on the association of those adverse events with NNAs, including dipyrone and NSAIDs.

All studies with a case-control or a cohort-study design that provided data to assess the excess mortality in the population studied were selected. For case-control studies the required data included estimates of the relative risk associated with drug exposure compared with non-exposure, the percentage of cases exposed to the drug, the overall incidence rate of the disease in the source population, and the case-fatality rate. Where the original article did not include all the necessary data, a Medline literature search was performed to locate auxiliary reports by the study investigators, containing estimates of the overall risk of disease in the study population or of the case fatality rates. For each study the excess mortality attributed to short-term use (a one-week period) was calculated by multiplying the estimate of the one-week excess risk by the case-fatality rate of the adverse event. One-week risks of disease in the general population were estimated from risk estimates for longer time periods, on the assumption of a constant risk of disease.

The following procedure was used to calculate from the case-control studies the one-week risk difference: the aetiological fraction (EF), i.e., the proportion in the study population of studied adverse events that could be attributed to specific NNA or NSAID use, was estimated by [(RR-1)/RR]Pe, where RR is the relative risk of the specific adverse event in the exposed (users of a specific drug) compared with the non-exposed (non-users of the drug) and Pe is the percentage of exposed cases (number of cases exposed to the drug/total number of cases).

Multivariate RR estimates, when provided, were used in the calculations. The risk of the adverse event in non-users (Ru) was calculated as (1-EF)RT, where RT is its overall weekly incidence in the study population. Its risk in users (Re) was calculated by multiplying the risk in the non-exposed by the estimated relative risk in the exposed, (Ru)(RR). The excess mortality was summed across adverse events to determine the overall excess mortality attributed to short-term use of each NNA. When more than one of the studies assessed the association between a drug and a given adverse event, the median excess mortality estimate for the drug was used.

Results[1]

Ten case-control studies contained the necessary information to calculate four adverse-event-specific excess mortality rates attributed to NNAs: one on anaphylaxis(1), one on agranulocytosis (2), one on aplastic anaemia (2), and seven on serious gastrointestinal complications, including haemorrhage and perforation (3-9). Only for dipyrone, propyphenazone, aspirin and

---

[1] Reference to the studies cited and the literature are found at the end of this case history.

diclofenac were relative risk estimates for all four adverse events given. Excess mortality rates were calculated for all NNAs (dipyrone, propyphenazone and paracetamol) and NSAIDs (aspirin, diclofenac, indomethacin and naproxen), which were investigated in at least one study of gastrointestinal complications.

Of the seven studies examining gastrointestinal complications, three (4, 7, 9) restricted the analyses to hospitalizations or deaths due to bleeding or perforated peptic ulcer, and another (8) provided data to evaluate bleeding due exclusively to peptic ulcer. For five studies (4-8) the estimates of the overall incidence or the case fatality of the gastrointestinal complications were obtained from auxiliary reports.

Anaphylaxis

Anaphylaxis is the maximum variant of an immediate type reaction that occurs in previously sensitized persons after re-exposure to the sensitizing antigen. A clinically indistinguishable syndrome which is not antibody-mediated and does not require previous exposure to the antigen is called an *anaphylactoid reaction*. The anaphylactic and anaphylactoid response appears usually within minutes of administration of the specific antigen. It is characterized by cutaneous, gastrointestinal, respiratory, cardiovascular or central-nervous symptoms that can occur either singly or in combination. Life-threatening conditions involve respiratory obstruction leading to respiratory failure or cardiovascular collapse or shock.

Only one study, in the Netherlands, provided the necessary data for the calculation of the excess mortality. It attributed to drugs 107 of 336 cases classified as probable or possible anaphylaxis, indicating an annual incidence of drug-induced anaphylaxis of 3.7 per million (107 cases in a two-year period in a population of 14.5 million). The multivariate RR estimates for anaphylaxis leading to hospital admission were given separately for 1987 and 1988. Therefore, a pooled estimate was calculated by the method outlined by Greenland (10). In the category "other analgesics," the authors included salicylic-acid derivatives, pyrazolones and dipyrone. The relative risk of these agents was assumed to be identical, therefore. The excess mortality from anaphylactic shock ranged from 0.001 per million for propyphenazone and paracetamol to 0.004 per million for diclofenac.

Agranulocytosis

Agranulocytosis, defined as a granulocyte reduction below $0.5 \times 10^9/L$, is associated with clinical symptoms of acute bacterial infections. Its initial manifestations are due to the severity, site (e.g., lungs, oropharynx, urinary tract or blood) and duration of the infection. Typical symptoms are fever and sore throat. Two mechanisms of drug-induced agranulocytosis have been proposed: immune and toxic. The immunological mechanism is correlated with rapid peripheral destruction of granulocytes in a previously sensitized patient. Drug-dependent antibodies adhere to circulating granulocytes, causing their abrupt destruction. The toxic type of the disease also leads to sudden destruction of granulocytes. However, this may occur after a latent period during which the patient receives a substantial amount of the causative drug resulting in damage to granulocyte precursors and mature peripheral granulocytes. There is considerable evidence that dipyrone-induced agranulocytosis is immune-mediated.

The International Agranulocytosis and Aplastic Anaemia Study (IAAAS) carried out a population-based case-control study in Germany, Italy, Hungary, Spain, Israel, Sweden and Bulgaria; it gave an overall annual incidence rate of community-acquired agranulocytosis of 3.4 per million (2). Estimates of annual incidence rates differed by geographic region. They were lowest in Milan (1.5 per million) and highest in Budapest (5.5 per million). In Uppsala, Sweden - where dipyrone was not available during the study period - the annual rate was 5.1 per million. Incidence rate was age-dependent and rose sharply with age. The overall case fatality rate was 10% (2). The excess mortality ranged from 0.0013 per million users of paracetamol and propyphenazone to 0.074 per million dipyrone users.

Aplastic anaemia

Aplastic anaemia refers to a diverse group of potentially severe bone-marrow disorders characterized by pancytopenia and a marrow largely devoid of haematopoietic cells. Its clinical features, such as bleeding manifestations, infections, fatigue and pallor, are the effects of too few functional peripheral blood cells. Its annual incidence rate associated with hospital admission is 2.0 per million (2). Fatality rates increase with age; the overall rate is 46% within two years (2). Marrow transplantation has dramatically improved survival, however. The excess mortality from the disease ranged from 0. 0032 per million aspirin users to 0.12 per million users of indomethacin.

Serious upper gastrointestinal complications

The mechanisms by which NSAIDs cause gastrointestinal injury are those dependent on cyclooxygenase inhibition and those that exert direct toxic effects on the local mucosa. A major protective mechanism against mucosal injury is the concentration of prostaglandin in the gastrointestinal mucosa; it is suppressed by inhibition of cyclooxygenase, the rate-limiting enzyme in the synthesis of prostaglandin. Aspirin inhibits it irreversibly, and most other NSAIDs reversibly.

Overall excess mortality

The overall excess mortality from anaphylaxis, agranulocytosis, aplastic anaemia and serious upper gastrointestinal complications was higher for NSAIDs than for other NNAs. The excess mortality associated with gastrointestinal complications was the principal influence on the overall estimate, contributing 99% of the excess mortality in users of all NSAIDs (aspirin, diclofenac, indomethacin and naproxen). The main influence on the overall mortality estimate among users of NNAs was gastrointestinal complications of treatment with paracetamol (96%) and dipyrone (69%). Propyphenazone contributed the least, showing no excess risk of gastro-intestinal complications.

Mortality per million users of NSAIDs was 2.0 for aspirin, 5.9 for diclofenac, 6.5 for naproxen and 11.7 for indomethacin. The rates for NNAs ranged from 0.002 for propyphenazone to 0.25 and 0.2 for paracetamol and dipyrone users, respectively (Table 1 and Figure 1).

Table 1: *Excess mortality per million short-term users, by adverse event*

	Agranulo-cytosis	Aplastic anaemia	Anaphylaxis	GI bleeding	(% of total)
Non-narcotics					
Dipyrone	0.074	0.000	0.002	0.171	(69%)
Propyphenazone	0.001	0.000	0.001	0.000	(0%)
Paracetamol	0.001	0.006	0.001	0.190	(96%)
NSAIDs					
Aspirin	0.006	0.003	0.002	2.018	(99%)
Diclofenac	0.000	0.054	0.004	5.857	(99%)
Indomethacin	0.035	0.120		11.576	(99%)
Naproxen	—	—	0.002	6.474	(>99%)

Discussion on risk assessment

The absolute risk of mortality associated with dipyrone appears to be substantially lower than that associated with NSAIDs for short-term relief of pain. For dipyrone the estimated excess mortality due to agranulocytosis, aplastic anaemia, anaphylaxis and serious upper gastrointestinal complications was 1.7 per million.

Figure 1. Overall mortality from short-term use of NNAs and NSAIDs (total)

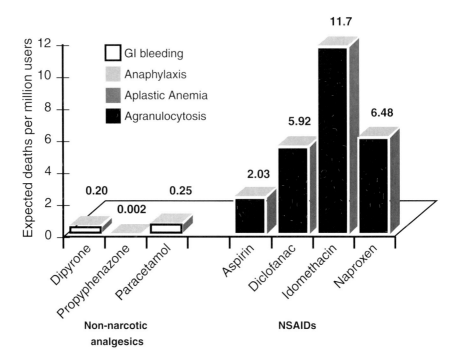

The overall excess mortality estimates were influenced largely by the excess mortality associated with upper gastrointestinal complications, an adverse event more commonly associated with NSAIDs, such as aspirin, diclofenac or naproxen, than with dipyrone, paracetamol or propyphenazone.

A limitation of this evaluation was the use of relative risk estimates that did not account for duration of therapy, drug dose, or previous therapy with the drugs under study. In this case it was assumed that the risk of adverse effects was constant throughout therapy, which is unlikely to be the case. Most anaphylactic reactions occur within one hour of exposure to a drug. The risk of gastrointestinal haemorrhage is highest early in NSAID therapy (within one month of initiation) and decreases over time. Prophylactic use of aspirin has been shown to increase the risk of peptic ulcer bleeding (1, 12). Patients who began treatment with aspirin one week before admission to hospital had an increased relative risk of 4.8, compared with a constant RR of 2.9 for aspirin intake begun between one week and three months before admission. Another limitation is that the published studies contained no information on indication for drug use. However, no hypotheses suggest any increased frequency of the studied adverse events in the treatment of fever, pain or inflammation.

Conclusions on risk assessment

To compare the adverse drug-attributed public-health impact of non-narcotic analgesics, an epidemiological perspective was chosen and the drug-related mortality quantified. Gastrointestinal complications accounted for most of the excess mortality in the overall estimate, for 99% of it among users of NSAIDs (aspirin, diclofenac, indomethacin and naproxen). They accounted for most also among those treated with propyphenazone and paracetamol. For dipyrone, gastrointestinal complications accounted for 69%, and agranulocytosis for 30%, of the overall excess mortality.

Benefit-Risk Assessment

The benefits of dipyrone are equivalent or superior to those of other non-narcotic analgesics. The relative risk of dipyrone-associated agranulocytosis is substantial but the excess risk is very small. Dipyrone carries a lower risk of fatal complications from potentially fatal adverse events than aspirin or other NSAIDs.

Options Analysis

New methods developed from a body of epidemiological studies showed that the risk of agranulocytosis had been overestimated in the 1970s and that the overall risk of dipyrone compared favourably with that of alternative analgesics. Although dipyrone was not protected by patent, Hoechst in 1994 decided to submit Novalgin (dipyrone) for re-approval in Sweden.

Decision-Making

In 1995, Sweden re-approved Novalgin 500 mg tablets and Novalgin solution for injection, 500 ml, for short-term treatment of acute moderate to severe pain after tissue injury (e.g., from surgical procedures) and acute moderate to severe colicky pain, in the urinary or biliary tract, for example.

Points Illustrated

Drug safety is often evaluated by determining the frequency of occurrence of one particular drug-associated adverse event. This assumes that all other adverse events have an identical profile and frequency. When this is not the case safety can be assessed only by a three-dimensional construct of the qualitative profile of adverse events, their frequency of occurrence, and a common measure of health outcome.

The purpose of the present evaluation was to estimate the adverse drug-attributed public-health effects of dipyrone and to compare them with those of other non-narcotic analgesics and non-steroidal anti-inflammatory drugs. Ideally, such an evaluation would take account of all known drug-attributed adverse events, their duration and frequency of occurrence, and their varying degrees of seriousness. To be meaningful, a comparative safety evaluation must employ an objective measure to incorporate and quantify the impact of all adverse events. Such a common outcome measure could depend on the perspective chosen, however.

The relative benefit-risk profile was evaluated from an epidemiological perspective. Death was chosen as the common outcome of the different adverse events, thereby restricting the evaluation to potentially life-threatening events. The drug-related mortality for dipyrone and other non-narcotic analgesics, as a measure of the adverse drug-attributed public-health impact, was estimated and expressed by the excess mortality.

References

(1) van der Klauw MM, Stricker BHC, Herings RMC, Cost WS, Valkenburg HA: A population based case-cohort study of drug-induced anaphylaxis. *Brit J Clin Pharmacol* 1993; 35: 400-408.

(2) Kaufman DW, Kelly JP, Levy M, Shapiro S: The drug aetiology of agranulocytosis and aplastic anaemia. *Monographs in Epidemiology and Biostatistics*. Vol.18, Oxford University Press, 1991.

(3) Laporte JR, Carné X, Vidal X, Moreno V, Juan J: Upper gastrointestinal bleeding in relation to previous use of analgesics and non-steroidal anti-inflammatory drugs. *Lancet* 1991, 337; 85-89.

(4) Langman MJS, Weil J, Wainwright P, *et al.*: Risks of bleeding peptic ulcer associated with individual non-steroid anti-inflammatory drugs. *Lancet* 1994; 343: 1075-1078.

(5) Henry D, Dobson A, Turner C: Variability in the risk of major gastrointestinal complications from non-aspirin anti-inflammatory drugs. *Gastroenter* 1993; 105: 1078-1088.

(6) Langman MJS, Coggon D, Spiegelhalter D: Analgesic intake and the risk of acute upper gastrointestinal bleeding. *American Journal of Medicine* 1983; 74: 79-82.

(7) Faulkner G, Pritchard P, Somerville K, Langman MJS: Aspirin and bleeding peptic ulcers in the elderly. *BMJ* 1988; 297: 1311-1313.

(8) Needham CD, Kyle J, Jones PF, Johnston SJ, Kerridge DF: Aspirin and alcohol in gastrointestinal haemorrhage. *Gut* 1971; 12: 819-821.

(9) Armstrong CP, Blower AL: Non-steroidal anti-inflammatory drugs and life-threatening complications of peptic ulceration. *Gut* 1987; 28: 527-532.

(10) Grenland S: Quantitative methods in the review of epidemiologic literature. *Epidemiologic reviews* 1987; 9: 1-30.

(11) Weil J, Colin-Jones D, Langman M, Lawson D, Logan R, Murphy M, Rawlins M, Vessey M, Wainwright P: Prophylactic aspirin and peptic ulcer bleeding. *BMJ* 1995; 310: 827-830.

(12) Slattery J, Warlow CP, Shorrock CJ, MJS Langman: Risks of gastrointestinal bleeding during secondary prevention of vascular events with aspirin — Analysis of gastrointestinal bleeding during the UK-TIA Trial. *Gut* 1995; 37: 509-511.

4. Temafloxacin

Background

Temafloxacin, a fluoroquinolone used most widely in the United States, where it was first approved in January 1992, was also available in the United Kingdom, Germany and Sweden. It was no more efficacious than other fluoroquinolones.

Risk

In the United States it appeared to be associated with a higher rate of spontaneous reporting than other fluoroquinolones. Reported events included disseminated intravascular coagulation (DIC), haemolytic anaemia, thrombocytopenia, renal impairment and hypoglycaemia. Apart from hypoglycaemia, which occurred predominantly in the elderly, it was not possible to predict a high-risk group for the other reactions.

In Sweden, where temafloxacin was launched in September 1991, an estimated 30,000 patients had received it through May 1992. During that time it accounted for 36 spontaneous reports of medically important adverse reactions possibly or probably connected with it. None referred to hypoglycaemia but three were of anaphylactoid reactions; no drug-related death was reported. Also, several cases of acute haemolysis/haemolytic anaemia were reported, and one 70-year-old male developed haemolytic uraemic syndrome with DIC. The overall adverse-reaction reporting rate (> 1 case per 1000 patients) was unprecedented for an antibiotic in Sweden.

Analysis of risk

Temafloxacin and three other fluoroquinolones were the subjects of a comparative safety analysis undertaken of spontaneous reports received in the United States during the first 120 days post-approval. IMS data were used for denominators. The reporting rate for temofloxacin was 108/100,000 prescriptions, compared with 13, 25 and 20 per 100,000 for the other three drugs. Intensive review of the comparator fluoroquinolones revealed none of the serious reactions associated with temofloxacin. The differences could not be attributed to reporting bias or publicity; they were possibly related directly to the chemical structure of temofloxacin.

Outcome

The company together with the Food and Drug Administration agreed to withdraw temafloxacin in the United States in June 1992. It was withdrawn worldwide at the same time.

Points illustrated

A carefully controlled analysis showed that important information and consequences can be ascertained from spontaneous-report data that show especially large differences between products. A transcript of the FDA Advisory Committee proceedings is available. The case is also documented in papers in the literature.*

5. Remoxipride

Summary

Remoxipride, (Roxiam), an antipsychosis agent of the benzamide group, was approved in Sweden in January 1991 for the treatment of schizophrenia and other types of psychosis in which the classical neuroleptics were found to cause intolerable side-effects. Remoxipride was approved in most European countries shortly afterwards. In the clinical trials it was found to be as effective as haloperidol, chlorpromazine and thioridazine. Its main advantages were that it caused significantly fewer extrapyramidal symptoms (EPS) than haloperidol and less sedation and anticholinergic adverse effects than chlorpromazine and thioridazine. In general, patients tolerated it well and it penetrated the market quickly.

In August 1993 the company informed regulatory agencies of four cases of aplastic anaemia and during the next four months four more cases were identified. Two of the eight patients died of the blood dyscrasia. The estimated incidence of aplastic anaemia varied between countries from 0 in 15,000 patients in Germany to 2 in 16,000 in Sweden and 5 in 10,000-12,000

---

* Norrby, S.R. and Leitman, P.S. Fluoroquinolone toxicities: update. *Drugs*, 45 (Supplement 3):59-64, 1993. Also, Finch, R.G. Withdrawal of temafloxacin: are there implications for other quinolones? *Drug Safety*, 8: 9-11, 1993.

in the United Kingdom. In all, 50,000 patients were estimated to have been exposed to the drug, yielding a rate of 1 fatal reaction in 25,000 patients. The Swedish Medical Product Agency (MPA) evaluated the risk with aplastic anaemia as acceptable but the Committee for Proprietary Medicinal Products (CPMP) gave a negative opinion and the company withdrew the product from the world market in February 1994. This document is in itself a summation and update of the benefit-risk evaluation done by the MPA (Sweden) in December 1993.

Schizophrenia: occurrence, and related morbidity and mortality

Schizophrenia is a widespread disease, occurring all over the world and in all kinds of societies. Its annual incidence in the age-groups 15 years and over is around 1 per 1000 population. Life-time prevalence is about 1%, in men and women alike. Around 2 million new cases are diagnosed annually worldwide. The peak onset occurs between 15 and 25 years of age in men and somewhat later in women. Onset is rarely before 10 or after 50 years of age. Early onset is considered particularly ominous. Irrespective of the attitude adopted by society, whether these patients are treated as hospital inpatients or mainly at outpatient clinics, schizophrenia is responsible for a substantial part of the costs of health care.

Schizophrenic symptoms may be divided into positive (including thought disorder, loose associations, hallucinations, bizarre behaviour) and negative (affective blunting, poverty of speech, anhedonia and lack of motivation, social withdrawal). These two categories of symptoms differ with regard to their amenability to medical treatment.

Patients with schizophrenia run a considerable risk of premature death, mainly due to suicide. About 50% attempt suicide and10% succeed. On a yearly basis three to five of every 1000 schizophrenic patients commit suicide. Because of their poor rapport with both friends and therapists these suicides are often unpredictable. There is some evidence that patients who develop akathisia also may exhibit aggressive behaviour, including suicide.

During a phase of marked exacerbation of schizophrenic symptoms there is sometimes a rise in body temperature with elevated levels of plasma urea and increasing muscular rigidity, and the patient may die of lethal catatonia. These cases are difficult to distinguish from the neuroleptic malignant syndrome, which has contributed to making such crises more common since the introduction of neuroleptics.

Whether patients with schizophrenia are at increased risk of somatic diseases (including pulmonary tuberculosis) remains uncertain. Increased general morbidity could probably be ascribed to environmental factors in the old mental hospitals, but even recent linkage-studies have continued to show an excess of both natural and unnatural deaths.

General treatment

The introduction of neuroleptic therapy in the mid-1950s brought a major change in schizophrenic symptomatology as well as in the quality of life of patients. Today, 25% seem to recover completely and another 25% partially, being able to support themselves at a lower level than before they became ill. Around 50% remain significantly impaired for the rest of their lives.

Although neuroleptic treatment has made it possible to discharge patients, there are several reasons for non-compliance with this medical treatment: patients deny their symptoms, and they suffer from such unpleasant side-effects as rigidity, akathisia, sedation, orthostatism and sexual disturbances. Neuroleptics have been particularly effective in the modification of positive symptoms, but they have less effect on negative symptoms and sometimes even aggravate them.

Improvements claimed for new antipsychotic drugs have been linked mainly with allegedly improved effects on negative symptoms and to beneficial effects in a therapy-resistant group of patients with schizophrenia. Evidence has suggested also an improved safety profile with regard to the induction of syndromes related to the extrapyramidal system.

Drug benefits

Shortly after remoxipride (Roxiam) was approved in Sweden in January 1991, it was approved in several other European countries (Denmark, Germany, Luxembourg and the United Kingdom). Remoxipride differs from the classical neuroleptic drugs mainly in having a shorter half-life, normally 4-7 h, and less affinity for muscarinic, serotonergic, alpha-adrenergic and histaminergic receptors. Like most other neuroleptic drugs (and anti-depressants), remoxipride is metabolized by cytochrome P450 CYP2D6, which exerts genetic polymorphism. About 7% of Caucasians are of the slow-metabolizer phenotype. The plasma half-life is about doubled in such individuals, as it is also among elderly patients and in patients with severely decreased renal function. The plasma concentration may also be increased by concomitant treatment with neuroleptics that are metabolized by the same enzyme and which have higher affinity to the enzyme than remoxipride, while remoxipride will probably not increase the plasma concentrations of such substances.

Comparisons in clinical trials

In the clinical trials remoxipride was compared mostly with haloperidol but also in a few studies with thioridazine and chlorpromazine. No difference was found in efficacy between remoxipride and haloperidol, thioridazine or chlorpromazine. In general, remoxipride had been well tolerated and shown to have a significantly lower incidence of sedative effects than haloperidol, and a two- to three-fold lower incidence of extrapyramidal side-effects, including akathisia. The drop-out rate because of adverse effects (3.3%) was significantly lower than for haloperidol (14%), as was the need for anticholinergic treatment. Remoxipride was also significantly less sedative than chlorpromazine and thioridazine, and had fewer autonomic side-effects such as hypotension, obstipation and blurred vision.

In the clinical trials programme, which covered about 2500 patients exposed to remoxipride, and in clinical practice, with an estimated 50,000 exposed patients, the adverse-reaction profile of remoxipride was found to be favourable until the occurrence of aplastic anaemia.

The risk with remoxipride

In August 1993 the company informed the MPA of three cases of aplastic anaemia, and on 27 September 1993 reported a total of four cases in the United Kingdom. Until then there were no such reports in Sweden. The MPA asked the old network of the International Aplastic Anaemia and Agranulocytosis Study to search the patient registers and all haematology-pathology registers; a "dear doctor" letter was sent to all haematologists, asking for information on all cases of confirmed or suspected aplastic anaemia occurring between 1 January 1991 and 30 August 1993. Nurse monitors were sent to check all case records for (a) a psychiatric history, and (b) a history of neuroleptic drug intake. An experienced pathologist reviewed all suspected cases. By 18 October, all cases had been analysed. In none of the 26 cases of confirmed aplastic anaemia (and in none of the 15 suspected cases) was there any indication of exposure to remoxipride. Two patients had been exposed to other neuroleptics.

However, two cases were reported to the Northern Regional Pharmacovigilance Centre during the survey: a woman hospitalized on 1 September and a man on 16 September. Bone-marrow samples were obtained quickly from both patients and a serum sample from the first. During the actual period an estimated 16,000 patients had been treated with remoxipride.

From September through December four more cases of aplastic anaemia were identified: two in Sweden, one in Luxembourg and one more in the United Kingdom. These, in addition to the four reported in the United Kingdom in August and September (see above), made eight cases, of whom two died from the blood dyscrasia. The estimated incidence of aplastic anaemia varied between countries from 0 in 15,000 patients in Germany, 2 in 16,000 patients in Sweden to 5 in 10,000-12,000 in the UK. In all, 50,000 patients were estimated to have been exposed to the drug, yielding a rate of one fatal reaction in 25,000 patients.

The comparators

It was possible to compare remoxipride with haloperidol and the older neuroleptic drugs chlorpromazine, thioridazine and perphenazine.

The risk profiles

The following table shows the profile of adverse reactions reported in Sweden in relation to sales.

The incidence is calculated by dividing the number of reports with a possible relation between drug and reaction by person-years under exposure, estimated by dividing by 365 the total annual sales figures, using a defined daily dose (sales figures were available only up to 30 June 1993).

Comparative benefit-risk evaluation

Schizophrenia is a relatively common and very serious chronic disease with substantial disease-related morbidity and mortality. On a lifetime basis it has been reported that 50% of patients attempt suicide and that about 10% die of suicide. On a yearly basis 3-5/1000 patients commit suicide. Such suicides often occur during psychotic phases and are difficult to predict. Therefore, control of the psychosis and prevention of relapse are of major importance to reduce disease-related mortality. Even modern treatment is only partially successful. About 25% of patients are estimated to recover completely and another 25% partially, while 50% remain significantly impaired for the rest of their lives. A most important aim in the maintenance of treatment and avoidance of relapse is to secure that patients continue treatment as long as it is necessary. With the current trend in the management of mental illness to minimize long-term hospitalization, much of the success depends on how well the patient accepts the treatment.

Reports of adverse reactions to neuroleptics in Sweden through 30 June 1993 (per 10,000 patient-years exposure)

	Chlorpromazine	Haloperidol	Thioridazine	Clozapine	Remoxipride
Total # reports	136	122	129	155	70
Total person years	110,010	226,567	232,419	9,320	9,567
Total # deaths	6 (0.6)	5 (0.2)	7 (0.3)	7 (7.5)	1 (1.1)
Neutropenia	1 (0.1)	1 (0.0)	1 (0.0)	2.1 (2.8)	0 (0.0)
Leukopenia	3 (0.3)	1 (0.0)	2 (0.1)	4 (4.3)	1 (1.1)
Agranulocytosis	13 (1.2)	7 (0.3)	15 (0.7)	39 (42)	0 (0.0)
Pancytopenia	0 (0.0)	1 (0.0)	1 (0.0)	1 (1.1)	0 (0.0)
Aplastic anemia	0 (0.0)	0 (0.0)	0 (0.0)	0 (0.0)	2 (2.1)
Thrombo-cytopenia	2 (0.2)	0 (0.0)	5 (0.2)	4 (4.3)	2 (2.1)
Haematologic ADRs	22 (2.2)	14 (0.6)	28 (1.2)	100 (1.7)	5 (5.2)
Liver reactions	63 (5.7)	15 (0.7)	19 (0.8)	9 (9.7)	2 (2.1)
ECG changes/ Arrhythmias	2 (0.2)	2 (0.1)	10 (0.4)	5 (5.4)	0 (0.0)
Sudden death	0 (0.0)	0 (0.0)	3 (0.1)	1 (1.1)	0 (0.0)
Tardive dyskinesia	12 (1.1)	18 (0.8)	16 (0.7)	0 (0.0)	0 (0.0)
Neuroleptic malignant syndrome	2 (0.2)	16 (0.7)	3 (0.1)	0 (0.0)	2 (2.1)
Acute dystonia	4 (0.4)	7 (0.3)	0 (0.0)	0 (0.0)	15 (15.7)

Fatal reactions:

Chlorpromazine	6 (5 agranulocytosis)
Haloperidol	5 (1 agranulocytosis, 1 pancytopenia)
Thioridazine	7 (4 agranulocytosis, 3 sudden death)
Clozapine	7 (4 of 39 cases of agranulocytosis, 1 myocarditis, 1 sudden death, and 1 pulmonary oedema)
Remoxipride	1 (aplastic anaemia, probably only thrombocytopenia peripherally)

The antipsychosis drugs available in Sweden belong to several different chemical groups. Perphenazine and haloperidol dominate but thioridazine is also common. Remoxipride has been shown to be as effective as haloperidol and thioridazine. Remoxipride is less sedative than both of these drugs and has significantly fewer extrapyramidal symptoms, including akathisia. than haloperidol. It has fewer autonomic as well as cardiac side-effects than thioridazine. In general, remoxipride has high patient acceptability, which is important for the possibility of maintenance of treatment.

From available data it seems clear that the different antipsychosis drugs have individual profiles of adverse effects but, for a thorough evaluation of their comparative risks, additional data were needed, especially on the risk of serious reactions from the older drugs. In Sweden, remoxipride was the only available drug in the new group of substituted benzamides. Sulpiride, which is chemically close, was not approved because of problems in the toxicological documentation, and risperidone had not yet been approved.

The benefits of clozapine are well-documented in refractory schizophrenia, as are the high risks of agranulocytosis, sedation and seizures, and there is no doubt that it is a valuable drug in selected cases. With an incidence of agranulocytosis of 0.5% and a case fatality rate of 9%, the risk of fatal agranulocytosis from clozapine is of the order of 1 per 2000-3000 patients.

At that time, the risk of aplastic anaemia from remoxipride seemed high, but the risk of fatal reactions did not seem higher than that from alternative drugs or from pharmacotherapeutic strategies in general, for moderate to serious disease.

Indeed, if the drop-out rates from clinical trials are considered, more than four times as many patients taking haloperidol as those taking remoxipride would stop their treatment prematurely and then run an increased risk of suicide.

Consequently, it did not seem warranted to withdraw remoxipride from the Swedish market; rather, its indications were restricted. For patients who did not tolerate the side-effects of the other available antipsychosis drugs the risk of the disease was judged to outweigh that of aplastic anaemia from remoxipride. A strict programme of blood monitoring was recommended for such patients, including measurements of haemoglobin, thrombocytes and white blood cells (including a differential count). Such a system has worked well for patients treated with clozapine and it should be possible to use it also for patients on remoxipride. It was judged possible to limit the damage to the bone marrow by early withdrawal of the drug but it could not be guaranteed that the aplastic anaemia would not progress.

6. Clozapine

Background

Clozapine, a tricyclic dibenzodiazepine, was developed by Sandoz-Wander in the late 1950s for the treatment of schizophrenia. Between 1972 and 1975 it was approved and marketed in many European countries and in South America. During this time isolated cases of granulocytopenia were reported to the company.

In February 1975 the drug was launched in Finland. Within six months 20 cases of suspected blood dyscrasias were reported among the estimated 3000 treated patients. Nine died, eight of agranulocytosis and one of acute leukaemia.

Benefit

Prior to 1975

From multiple open studies covering more than 1000 patients, investigators tended to conclude that clozapine was as efficacious as, or more efficacious than, standard neuroleptics such as perphenazine or chlorpromazine. Clozapine produced extrapyramidal effects less frequently than chlorpromazine.

Angst *et al.*, in a controlled clinical trial with a randomized double-blind parallel group of 64 patients receiving either clozapine 140 mg/day (average daily dose) or methotrimeprazine 180 mg/day (average daily dose) over four weeks, showed clozapine to be as efficacious as methotrimeprazine.

Ekblom and Haggstrom in a controlled clinical trial with a randomized double-blind parallel group of 41 schizophrenia patients receiving clozapine 310 mg/day (average daily dose) or chlorpromazine 365 mg/day (average daily dose) for six weeks showed clozapine to be as efficacious as chlorpromazine.

Fischer-Cornelssen *et al.*, in a random double-blind parallel-group, controlled multi-centre clinical trial of 217 schizophrenia patients receiving clozapine 300 mg/day (average daily dose) or chlorpromazine 360 mg (average daily dose) for six weeks, showed that clozapine had significantly higher efficacy than chlorpromazine.

Gerlach *et al.*, in a single-blind cross-over trial of 20 schizophrenia patients each receiving clozapine 200 mg (average daily dose) for 12 weeks followed by haloperidol 10 mg (average daily dose) for 12 weeks, showed clozapine to be significantly better than haloperidol.

Singer and Law, in a randomized double-blind parallel-group trial of 40 acute patients with acute schizophrenia receiving clozapine 155 mg (average daily dose) or chlorpromazine 200 mg (average daily dose), showed clozapine to be similar to chlorpromazine.

Vencovsky *et al.*, in a randomized double-blind parallel group trial with 52 schizophrenia patients receiving clozapine 300 mg (average daily dose) or chlorpromazine 600 mg (average daily dose), showed clozapine to be significantly better than chlorpromazine.

Chiu *et al.*, in a randomized double-blind parallel-group trial with 64 schizophrenia patients receiving clozapine 300 mg (average daily dose) or chlorpromazine 300 mg for six weeks, showed clozapine efficacy to be equivalent to that of chlorpromazine.

Fisher-Cornelsson and Ferner, in a randomized double-blind parallel-group trial with 723 schizophrenic patients receiving clozapine 300 mg or either chlorpromazine 350 mg, haloperidol 8 mg, trifluoperazine 30 mg or clopenthixol 100 mg for six weeks found clozapine to be significantly superior to haloperidol and clopenthixol, equivalent to chlorpromazine and significantly inferior to trifluoperazine.

In all the trials extrapyramidal effects were rare with clozapine.

After 1984

Claghorn *et al.* found that clozapine had significantly higher efficacy, but significantly fewer extrapyramidal side-effects, than chlorpromazine in a multi-centre randomized double-blind parallel-group trial with 124 schizophrenia patients with histories of tardive dyskinesia or extrapyramidal symptoms on previous therapy. Patients received either clozapine 370 mg (average daily dose) or chlorpromazine 740 mg (average daily dose) over four weeks.

Kane *et al.*, in a randomized double-blind parallel-group trial with 265 schizophrenia patients refractory to previous therapy, found clozapine to be significantly better, and to cause significantly fewer extrapyramidal symptoms, than chlorpromazine. The test drug was given for six weeks.

Risk

Frequency of clozapine agranulocytosis estimated by Sandoz-Wander *

In clinical trials (1962-1972)

Four cases of agranulocytosis occurred in 2900 patients — an estimated frequency of 1.4 per 1000. Agranulocytosis was defined as the presence of very few or no neutrophil granulocytes in the peripheral blood (granulocytopenia < 1600 neutrophils/mm^3).

Spontaneous reports from 1972 to August 1976

Country	Number of cases**	Fatal outcome	Calculated frequency per 1000 patients
Finland	16	8	7.09
Fed. Rep. Germany	15	6	0.38
Switzerland	12	6	0.63
Hungary	3	0	1.21
Yugoslavia	3	2	0.36
Austria	2	2	0.11
Denmark	2	1	1.35
South Africa	1	0	0.10
Total	54	25 (46%)	0.47

** The absolute numbers of cases of agranulocytosis and granulocytopenia reported. Average amount of clozapine used per patient = 24.2 g. This estimate was derived from sampling inpatient and outpatient prescribing practices. Amount of clozapine sold was derived from kilograms sold through May 31, 1976. Patient estimate = amount of clozapine sold in kg divided by 24.2.

Agranulocytosis as an adverse reaction to clozapine was found to occur most frequently during the first 18 weeks of treatment, similar in this respect to chlorpromazine. The following table shows the history of reports from 1954 to 1971 on various phenothiazines other than clozapine.

* From: Anderman and Griffith, Clozapine-Induced Agranulocytosis: A Situation Report up to August 1976, *Europ.J.Clin.Pharmacol.* 11, 199-201 (1977).

Frequency of cases of agranulocytosis related to various phenothiazines *

Author	Year	Number of cases	Denominator of usage	Estimated frequency/ 1000 patients
Giacombum	1954	1	147	6.8
Pollack	1955	2	2000	1.0
Goldman	1955	3	1000	3.0
Tuteur	1956	1	1508	0.66
Raskin	1957	3	625	4.8
Hippius	1958	2	1600	1.25
Fiore	1959	1	700	1.4
Ayd	1963	1	250000	0.004
Hollister	1964	1	3000-4000	ca. 0.34
Pisciotta	1969	1	1240	0.8
Litvak	1971	3	4200	0.7

* From: Anderman and Griffith, Clozapine-Induced Agranulocytosis: A Situation Report up to August 1976, *Europ.J.Clin.Pharmacol.* 11: 199-201 (1977)

Frequency of clozapine agranulocytosis estimated by the Finnish authorities

A total of 20 cases of suspected blood dyscrasias had been reported among an estimated 3000 patients; nine died, eight of agranulocytosis and one of acute leukaemia. Of the surviving cases, two had asymptomatic thrombocytopenia and 9 had neutropenia/agranulocytosis. The overall estimated incidence was 0.5% for agranulocytosis and 0.6% for neutropenia. Six patients had experienced neutropenia in connection with previous neuroleptic treatment. Only 25% of the cases occurred within 6 weeks; 75% occurred within 12 weeks and 25% after treatment for 12 weeks or more. Other than previous episodes of neutropenia, there were no special risk factors (J. Idänpään-Heikkilä, E. Alhava, M. Olkinuora and I.P. Palva. Agranulocytosis during treatment with clozapine. *Lancet*, 1975, No. II, p. 611).

Benefit-risk assessment

By 1977 the efficacy of clozapine was judged to be about equal to conventional therapy. The frequency of extrapyramidal reactions was less than for conventional treatment, which was regarded as a clear benefit. The risk of agranulocytosis was judged to be clearly higher than that of conventional therapy and the case fatality rate at that time was considered high. The discrepancy between the incidence estimates of agranulocytosis from clinical trials, 1.4 per 1000, and from the Finnish post-marketing experience, 5 per

126

1000, can be explained by the short duration of most trials (4-6 weeks). Only 25% of the cases reported in the post-marketing situation occurred within the first six weeks. The benefit-risk balance was judged differently in different countries and the drug was withdrawn from most, though not all, countries. Around 1985, clozapine was reintroduced in many countries since (a) it had been proven in further clinical trials that it was efficacious in about 30% of otherwise treatment-resistant patients, and (b) it was shown that regular blood monitoring could prevent the neutropenias from developing to agranulocytosis in most cases and virtually precluded a fatal outcome.

Action taken by the manufacturer

In response to the Finnish cases:

- All cases were investigated for the possibility of special susceptibility of the Finnish population.
- Information was sent to all regulatory authorities:
    - Information was sent to the medical community
    - Clozapine was withdrawn from the market in some countries (including France)
- Implementation of world-wide white blood cell monitoring made mandatory in each country where the drug continued to be marketed
- The "Ten Commandments for clozapine use" were developed
- Further investigations of the pathogenesis of clozapine-induced granulocytopenia were sponsored
- Promotion was stopped
- Clinical trials ceased temporarily
- Data gathered from the discontinued clinical trials were analysed
- Periodic updates were sent to regulatory authorities.

Points illustrated

The clinical trials were too short to detect the true frequency of this adverse reaction.

The initial trials had not been able to demonstrate the unique benefits of the drug before the Finnish epidemic of agranulocytosis but continued use and trials showed this later.

Continuous blood monitoring made it possible to decrease the risk of this type of agranulocytosis and especially to reduce the fatality rate.

7. Sparfloxacin

Background

Sparfloxacin is an antibiotic of the quinolone family. It has been marketed in France (September 1994), Luxembourg (November 1994), United Kingdom (December 1994), Denmark (January 1995), Belgium and Finland (March 1995). Introduction into the market was pending for some other Member States of the European Union, although the authorization had been granted (Austria, Germany, Greece, Ireland, Italy, Netherlands, Portugal, Sweden, United Kingdom). Sparfloxacin has been marketed also in Japan (August 1993), Morocco (February 1995), and the Philippines, Peru and Uruguay (April 1995).

Sparfloxacin is available as 100 mg and 200 mg film-coated tablets. There is no harmonized Summary of Product Characteristics (SPC) within the European Union or worldwide, particularly with regard to the approved indications and the labelling of undesirable effects, precautions and warnings.

In Japan, products containing sparfloxacin are indicated for the treatment of cutaneous, upper and lower respiratory, urogenital, hepato-biliary, digestive, ophthalmological and stomatological infections. In other countries the indications are more restricted. As an example, in two member states of the European Union (France and Luxembourg) medicinal products containing sparfloxacin have been approved and marketed for the treatment in adults of:

- presumed community-acquired acute bacterial pneumonia, whether pneumococcal or non-pneumococcal
- exacerbation of chronic obstructive pulmonary disease (COPD)
- purulent acute sinusitis.

The medicine is given in a single-dose regimen of 400 mg as a loading dose on the first day, followed by 200 mg/ day as maintenance in a 10-day treatment of infections of the lower respiratory tract and for about four days for sinusitis. The drug was used mainly for the treatment of sinusitis ($\sim 60\%$), bronchitis (COPD ~ 20-22%) and pneumonia (~ 3-5%).

The issue prompting the risk-benefit evaluation

After eight months of marketing sparfloxacin-containing medicinal products in France, many more reports of serious phototoxic reactions were being received about them than about other fluoroquinolones. Therefore, in

May 1995 France issued a pharmacovigilance rapid alert related to 371 case reports received, of which 80% concerned cutaneous reactions.

In June 1995, Denmark referred its concern about the safety of the drug to the European Agency for the Evaluation of Medicinal Products (EMEA) and asked the Committee on Proprietary Medicinal Products (CPMP) for an opinion on the risks and benefits of products containing sparfloxacin, in accordance with Article 12 of Directive 75/319/EEC.

Benefits

Sparfloxacin is an antibiotic for the treatment of infections caused by Gram-positive pathogens. It has very few alternatives for respiratory-tract infections caused by multi-resistant pneumococci. It has been the subject of a series of prospective, randomized and double-blind comparative trials.

The antibacterial spectrum of sparfloxacin combines the usual activity of a fluoroquinolone with an activity against *S. pneumoniae* at least two to four times higher than that of other antibiotics of its class. It is active also against respiratory infections caused by such pathogens as *H. influenzae, Mycoplasma pneumoniae,* and *Chlamydia*. A half-life of approximately 20 hours allows oral administration as a single daily dose, after a double loading dose.

Its efficacy has been demonstrated in patients with community-acquired pneumonia. It has been shown to be as efficacious as Augmentin and erythromycin in community-acquired pneumonia caused mainly by *S. pneumoniae* and *H. influenzae*.

Clinical equivalence has been demonstrated between sparfloxacin 200/100 mg (loading/maintenance dose) and Augmentin in acute exacerbation of chronic obstructive pulmonary disease (COPD).

For acute sinusitis, sparfloxacin at a dose of 400/200 mg four times a day for five days was as efficacious as cefuroxime axetil. No benefit was shown by increasing the daily dose.

Although it has not been claimed that urinary infections are indications for treatment with sparfloxacin, studies in some European countries have shown 200 mg sparfloxacin in a single dose to be as efficacious as ciprofloxacin for the treatment of acute gonococcal urethritis, and 200/100 mg for seven days to be as efficacious as seven-day treatment with doxycycline for non-gonococcal urethritis. No data are available for evaluating the effectiveness of sparfloxacin in general practice.

Risks

In general, the spectrum of spontaneously reported adverse reactions to sparfloxacin has been similar to that for other fluoroquinolones. They include phototoxicity, allergic reactions, muscle and joint pain, tendonitis, ruptured tendon, gastrointestinal disorders, headache, sleep disorders, hallucinations and dizziness. However, sparfloxin has been associated also with rare instances of the cardiac rhythm disorder known as *torsade de pointes*, and with a higher frequency of unexpectedly serious phototoxic reactions.

The increasing number of reports of serious cutaneous reactions became a matter of concern; 47% of the cutaneous reactions were phototoxic, such as sunburn-like eruptions on unprotected parts of the skin. They occurred even after treatment was discontinued. Of the reported cases, 25% had second-degree burns; about 6% were hospitalized and they recovered only slowly and sometimes with sequelae. Some of the differences in frequency of reporting of reactions to antibiotics of the quinolone family may be explained partly by reporting bias (due, e.g., to publicity or to time on the market). However, within this class the association of sparfloxacin with phototoxity is of major concern, because:

- it occurs sometimes with minimal exposure to ultra-violet light
- there is a high frequency of severe cases with serious outcomes
- recovery is slow and in some cases problems persist or recur long after the withdrawal of the drug.

As phase I studies have shown, phototoxic reactions are dose-dependent.

The other particular concern is cardiotoxicity. However, cardiotoxicity is unlikely to have major clinical consequences except in the case of inpatients with known risk factors such as underlying cardiac disease or treatment with drugs that prolong the Q-T interval. Q-T prolongation is a rare dose-related reaction.

The pathophysiology of the phototoxicity has not been elicited. Moreover, there is so far no evidence to clarify whether sparfloxacin has photomutagenic or photocarcinogenic properties.

Benefit-risk evaluation

The overall benefit-risk evaluation takes into account the safety profile, the efficacy profile, and the use of the drug in everyday medical practice in the general population. Thus the evaluation balances two factors: the association of the drug with a reaction that is not a common class-effect of fluoroquinolones and with a higher frequency of expected adverse reactions than other fluoroquinolones; and the use of the drug for the indications for which physicians in France primarily prescribe it.

Sinusitis (~60%)

The analysis of prescribing data has shown that sparfloxacin was prescribed in "all types of sinusitis" without distinction, and that about 30% of cases for which it was prescribed had been wrongly diagnosed. Because of the efficacy of sparfloxacin against pneumococci resistant to penicillin, the risk of inducing resistance to it by the use of suboptimal doses, and the higher risk of inducing serious cutaneous adverse reactions, the risk-benefit balance was regarded as favourable only for cases of acute sinusitis shown to be, or suspected of being, due to pneumococcal strains resistant to penicillin or other antibiotics.

Chronic obstructive pulmonary disease (COPD) (~20-22%)

The relevance of antibiotic therapy in this disease has been widely debated. Antibiotics are only beneficial in COPD with a certain degree of obstruction. However, in everyday medical practice the degree of obstruction is often unknown, because of the absence of respiratory-function test results. Besides, the treatment is often presumptive since the bacterial aetiology is generally undefined. There is no standard therapy and numerous therapeutic alternatives (including non-antibiotic treatment) have demonstrated efficacy in this disease. Also, acute exacerbation of infections in chronic bronchitis is fairly common and there is a risk of selection of resistant bacterial strains if treatment is often given in suboptimal doses. Thus, the choice of antibiotic must take safety into account, and therefore the risk-benefit balance in respect of sparfloxacin-containing medicinal products may be unfavourable.

Pneumonia (~3-5%)

Although this indication was the most thoroughly evaluated in the pre-marketing clinical trials, it accounts for a limited prescription volume, at least in France. These patients are generally bedridden and are therefore the least exposed to UV radiation, compared with all patients receiving the treatment for the other indications. However, the risk-benefit evaluation may be favourable only in cases of radiologically-confirmed community-acquired acute pneumonia that has failed to respond to other antibiotic therapy.

Dosing considerations

From the point of view strictly of efficacy, the proposed dose of 200/100 mg in the treatment of COPD could be supported, but this lower dosage of sparfloxacin might increase the risk of selection of resistance due to sub-inhibitory concentrations and repeated courses of treatment in this patient group. The higher dosage used in pneumonia should therefore also be considered for acute exacerbation of chronic bronchitis.

Options analysis

According to Directive 75/319/ECCC Art.13 (4), a European Article 12 procedure has three possible outcomes, which are binding on all Member States in the same way: withdrawal or suspension of the marketing authorization or variation of the Summary of Product Characteristics (SmPC). This last entails restrictions of indications, supply and use, or amendments to defined sections of the SmPC, such as contraindications, undesirable effects, precautions or warnings.

For sparfloxacin-containing medicinal products, despite the important risks associated with the drug the possible outcome is driven by the medical need of it, given that strains of S. pneumoniae are developing resistance at an increasing rate in some regions of the European Union.

However, the benefit-risk balance of sparfloxacin-containing medicinal products should be considered for each indication and dosing separately when deciding on the options for action.

Recommendation

Based on the evidence available, the CPMP was of the opinion that the use of sparfloxacin-containing medicinal products should be restricted to infections where no other treatment is available. It was decided that the medicinal product should only remain on the market if the conditions of marketing authorization were modified, further investigations were under-taken, and the SmPC was modified.

Indications

Sparfloxacin-containing medicinal products are indicated in the treatment of radiologically confirmed community acquired pneumonia which has failed to respond to conventional therapy and which either is caused by pneumococci highly resistant to penicillin (MIC ≥ 2 mg/l) and other antimicrobials, or occurs in an epidemiological environment indicating a high risk of such multiresistant strains.

The other indications were disallowed on grounds of the unfavourable benefit-risk balance.

200 mg strength

The selected dose regimen for the restricted indication is 400 mg as a single dose on the first day, followed by a 200 mg single dose daily for 10 days on average, and a maximum of 14 days.

100 mg strength

The CPMP was of the opinion that the marketing authorization of this formulation should be withdrawn, as this strength did not correspond to doses needed for the recommended indication. In addition, it increased the risk of misprescribing or non-compliance with the recommended pharmaceutical form for the recommended indication.

Further investigation

The CPMP was of the opinion that studies should be undertaken to investigate the photomutagenicity and photocarcinogenicity of sparfloxacin. It recommended also six-monthly updates for two years on safety and efficacy.

Additional remarks

The European Commission accepted the recommendations of the CPMP and announced its decisions on the variation of the marketing authorization of 200 mg sparfloxacin tablets and on the withdrawal of the 100 mg sparfloxacin tablets on 7 May 1996 and 14 June 1996, respectively, in the Official Journal of the European Union (No. C188/5).

APPENDIX C

MODEL FOR QUANTIFICATION OF RISKS[*]

The objective of this model is to make comparison easier between products from the same therapeutic class but with possibly very different adverse reactions. It is based on the usual international criteria of seriousness: fatal outcome, hospitalization, incapacity, sequelae (life-threatening reactions are included in the first criterion since, if they are life-threatening, they must sometimes be fatal).

Comprehensive information on the safety of a drug, including all adverse reactions and their outcomes (number of fatalities, number and duration of hospitalizations or incapacity, number and severity of sequelae, etc.), would require a cohort of many thousands of patients, which is rarely available. In practice, when adverse reactions occur and are diagnosed, their incidence is estimated on the basis of spontaneous reporting, with its numerous biases, or of epidemiological studies.

To permit comparison between drugs with different adverse reactions, a classification of seriousness and incidence into a few categories is proposed, on the basis of experience with the drug or of medical knowledge. The chosen ranges or boundaries are arbitrary, but considered reasonable.

Fatal (F) or life-threatening (LF) outcome: three categories of frequency

F (LF) $\geq 10\%$ of cases

$1\% \leq$ F (LF) $< 10\%$ of cases

F (LF) $< 1\%$ of cases

Hospitalization (H): two categories, according to duration

H ≤ 48 hours

H > 48 hours

Transient incapacity (I): two categories, according to duration

I ≤ 7 days

I > 7 days

Permanent sequelae (disability): evaluated according to standard scales

$\leq 20\%$ of cases

$> 20\%$ of cases

---

[*] Proposed by Christian Bénichou, MD (Synthélabo, Paris, France)

According to these data, a classification of seriousness into six categories is proposed, as follows:

Category 6:   Fatal outcome in more than 10% of cases (e.g., TEN)

Category 5:   Fatal outcome between 1 and 10% (e.g., hepatocellular injury, agranulocytosis, anaphylactic shock)

Category 4:   Fatal outcome <1%, permanent sequelae ≥20%

Category 3:   Hospitalization >2 days or incapacity >7 days

Category 2:   Hospitalization ≤2 days or incapacity ≤7 days

Category 1:   All other outcomes (of less intensity/severity)

The possible classifications can be shown as a grid.

	Fatal or life-threatening outcome	Sequelae	Hospi-talization	Incapacity	Other outcomes
Category 6	≥10%				
Category 5	1 to 10%				
Category 4	<1%	>20%			
Category 3		≤20%	>48 h	>7 d	
Category 2			≤48 h	≤7 d	
Category 1					X

Classification of incidence

Category 5 (very common):   >10 % (>10/100)

Category 4 (common or frequent):   between 10% and 1% (10/100 to 1/100)

Category 3 (uncommon or infrequent): between 1% and 0.1% (1/100 to 1/1000)

Category 2 (rare):   between 0.1% and 0.01% (1/1000 to 1/10,000)

Category 1 (very rare):   <0.01% (<1/10,000)

Global quantification of risks

Combining seriousness scores that can range from 6 to 1 and incidence scores from 5 to 1, a reaction score from 1 (1 x 1) to 30 (6 x 5) would result for each reaction; then an addition of reaction scores for all identified reactions could give a global drug risk score.

Clearly, such a scheme requires testing and validation, with special attention to the multifactorial aspects of the categorization scale for seriousness.

APPENDIX D

DETAILED EXAMPLE OF A QUANTITATIVE
BENEFIT-RISK EVALUATION: DIPYRONE[*]

I. BACKGROUND

Dipyrone belongs to the class of non-narcotic analgesics that have no anti-inflammatory action. It is effective for the treatment of fever and pain and is used in more than 100 countries, including Germany, France, Spain, Italy and Finland.

Dipyrone was introduced into clinical therapy in 1922 and registered in Sweden in 1934 for the treatment of various states of acute pain. Because of an apparently unacceptable risk of agranulocytosis, it was withdrawn from the Swedish market in 1974 and the US market in 1977. At that time the number of spontaneous reports suggested a causal relationship between dipyrone and agranulocytosis, though no reliable estimate of the overall incidence rate of agranulocytosis was available.

To obtain population-based evidence of the adverse public health impact of dipyrone, the International Agranulocytosis and Aplastic Anaemia Study (IAAAS), the largest ever blood-dyscrasia study, was carried out between 1980 and 1986. It provided better estimates than any previously available from several countries of the overall incidence rate of agranulocytosis and its associated mortality.

The Study found that the overall incidence of agranulocytosis was extremely low and that the risk associated with dipyrone had been overestimated in the 1970s. Hoechst, therefore, in 1994, resubmitted an application for marketing approval of dipyrone in Sweden.

This appendix describes the evaluation used to estimate the adverse drug-attributed public-health effects of dipyrone and to compare them with those of other non-narcotic analgesics, including non-steroidal anti-inflammatory drugs (NSAIDs).

II. BENEFIT

In addition to its antipyretic activity, dipyrone is an effective oral and parenteral treatment for moderate to severe pain, including post-operative

---

[*] Courtesy of Carlos Martinez and Ernst Weidmann (Hoechst Marion Roussel), and Stephen Rietbrock (University of Cologne).

pain. Oral dipyrone is superior to paracetamol and comparable to aspirin. In its parenteral form it compares in analgesic efficacy to the NSAIDs and to weak opioids.

III. RISK EVALUATION

A. Materials and Methods of the Benefit-Risk Evaluation

The benefit-risk evaluation was performed for competing treatment strategies for the indication of acute mild and moderate pain. The following analgesics and doses were selected: paracetamol ≤ 1500 mg/d, dipyrone ≤ 1500 mg/d, aspirin < 1000 mg/d, ibuprofen ≤ 1500 mg/d and diclofenac ≤ 100 mg/d. Acute pain was defined as requiring analgesic treatment for less than one week. Two age-groups were analysed: below 60 years, and 60 and above.

All potentially fatal adverse events reported with non-opioid analgesics were identified: anaphylaxis, Stevens-Johnson syndrome (SJS), toxic epidermal necrolysis (TEN), agranulocytosis, aplastic anaemia, upper gastrointestinal complications (haemorrhage or perforation), toxic liver disease, and end-stage renal failure. The Medline database was searched for all English-language reports of epidemiological studies published between January 1970 and February 1997 on the association of those adverse events with the use of non-narcotic analgesics.

All studies with a case-control or a cohort-study design that provided data to assess the excess mortality in the population studied were selected. The required data from the case-control studies were expected to provide information specific to the drugs and to the adverse events.

Drug-specific data included estimates of the relative risk of an adverse event associated with drug exposure compared with those associated with non-exposure (for gastrointestinal complications, dose-specific relative risk estimates were necessary), and the percentage of cases exposed to the drug. Information specific to adverse events comprised the incidence rate of the disease in the source population and the case-fatality rates of the adverse events. Age-specific estimates were essential for inclusion in the age sub-group analyses.

Drug-specific multivariate relative risk estimates (RR) from each study were combined, assuming a random effect of all estimates, and calculated according to the method of DerSimonian and Laird (1). Aetiological

138

fractions (*EF*), non-aetiological fractions (*NEF*) and the excess incidence rates (*EIR*) were calculated from the following equations:

$$EF = \frac{RR-1}{RR} P_{exposed}$$

$$NEF = \left\{ 1 - \frac{RR-1}{RR} P_{exposed} \right\}$$

$$EIR = IR \left\{ 1 - \frac{RR-1}{RR} P_{exposed} \right\} (RR-1)$$

where the incidence rate (*IR*) is the arithmetic mean of adverse event-specific incidence rates, and $P_{exposed}$ the arithmetic mean of the prevalence of exposure among cases from different studies. The last equation is derived from the common expression: *Excess Incidence = Incidence among exposed (IRxNEFxRR) – Incidence among non-exposed (IRxNEF)(3)*.

To address the problem of assessing and comparing different types of adverse events, a unique health-outcome measure was required which attached a weight (w_j) to each adverse event to facilitate the comparison. Therefore, case fatality rates specific to adverse events were selected as the unique health-outcome measure. The case fatality rate is the proportion of fatal cases of those who develop an illness. The arithmetic mean was used to estimate adverse-event-specific weights from all suitable studies.

The global excess risk (GER) due to different adverse events with weights w_j (common health outcome) was defined as the sum of drug-attributed weighted excess incidence rates of all considered adverse events.

$$GER = \sum_i w_i\, EIR_i$$

Because of different distributions, i.e., lognormal and normal distribution functions, confidence intervals could not be calculated with standard methods. Therefore, 95% confidence intervals for the drug-attributed excess mortality and for the global excess risks were determined by Monte Carlo simulation (2). Arithmetic means of simulated values were defined as point estimates.

B. Results

A total of 16 epidemiological studies provided information to calculate the global excess risk attributed to non-opioid analgesics: two on anaphylaxis (3, 4), one on agranulocytosis (5), one on aplastic anaemia (5), three on Stevens-Johnson syndrome (SJS) and toxic epidermal necrolysis (TEN) (6-8), and 10 on serious gastrointestinal complications, including upper GI haemorrhage and perforation (9-18). Two studies which addressed liver toxicity were identified, but they did not fulfil the inclusion criteria (19, 20). Excess mortality rates were calculated for dipyrone, paracetamol and three NSAIDs — aspirin, diclofenac and ibuprofen.

Of the 10 studies on gastrointestinal complications, five provided information on the overall incidence rate (9-13) and five on the case fatality rate (9, 13, 14, 17, 18); three provided relative risk estimates for the medicines (14-16).

Anaphylaxis

Anaphylaxis is the maximum variant of an immediate type reaction that occurs in previously sensitized persons after re-exposure to the sensitizing antigen. A clinically indistinguishable syndrome which is not antibody-mediated and does not require previous exposure to the antigen is called *an anaphylactoid reaction*. The anaphylactic or anaphylactoid response appears usually within minutes of administration of the specific antigen. It is characterized by cutaneous, gastrointestinal, respiratory, cardiovascular or central-nervous symptoms that can occur either singly or in combination. Life-threatening conditions involve respiratory obstruction leading to respiratory failure or cardiovascular collapse or shock.

Only one study provided the necessary data for the calculation of the excess mortality incidence rate, indicating an annual incidence of drug-induced anaphylaxis of 0.18 per million per week (252 cases in a two-year period in a population of 14.5 million) (3). In the category called "other analgesics" the authors included salicylic-acid derivatives, pyrazolones and dipyrone. Therefore, the relative risk of these agents was assumed to be identical. One study estimated a case fatality rate of 1.6% (4). Because of missing data age-specific excess mortality rates could not be determined. The weekly excess mortality from anaphylaxis ranged from 0.007 per million for dipyrone and aspirin users to 0.016 per million for diclofenac users.

Stevens-Johnson syndrome and toxic epidermal necrolysis (SJS/TEN)

SJS and TEN are severe skin reactions characterized by erythema and blisters or erosions of the skin or mucous membranes. In SJF, blisters cover less than 10% of the body surface, and in TEN more than 30%. Cases with

10 to 30% of skin detachment are classified as "SJS/TEN overlap"(6). 17.1 percent of all SJS/TEN cases are fatal: 4% of SJS, 25% of SJS/TEN overlap, and 36% of TEN (7). Death results from sepsis and renal failure (7).

The first results of an international case-control study of serious cutaneous adverse reactions (SCAR) performed in France, Germany, Italy, and Portugal have been published (6). This is the only study allowing the calculation of SJS/TEN-specific excess mortality rates for non-narcotic analgesics, including NSAIDs. The annual incidence rate of SJS/TEN in the community is estimated to be 1.82 per million (8). Because of missing data, age-specific excess mortality rates could not be determined.

Agranulocytosis

Agranulocytosis, defined as a granulocyte reduction below 0.5×10^9/L, is associated with clinical symptoms of acute bacterial infections. Its initial manifestations are due to the severity, site (e.g., lungs, oropharynx, urinary tract or blood) and duration of the infection. Typical symptoms are fever and sore throat. Two mechanisms of drug-induced agranulocytosis have been proposed: immune and toxic. The immunological mechanism is correlated with rapid peripheral destruction of granulocytes in a previously sensitized patient. Drug-dependent antibodies adhere to circulating granulocytes, causing their abrupt destruction. The toxic type of the disease also leads to sudden destruction of granulocytes. However, this may occur after a latent period during which the patient receives a substantial amount of the causative drug and granulocyte precursors and mature peripheral granulocytes are damaged. There is considerable evidence that dipyrone-induced agranulocytosis is immune-mediated.

The International Agranulocytosis and Aplastic Anaemia Study (IAAAS) carried out a population-based case-control study in Germany, Italy, Hungary, Spain, Israel, Sweden and Bulgaria; it gave an overall annual incidence rate of community-acquired agranulocytosis of 3.4 per million (5). Estimates of annual incidence rates differed by geographic region. They were lowest in Milan (1.5 per million) and highest in Budapest (5.5 per million). In Uppsala, Sweden - where dipyrone was not available during the study period - the annual rate was 5.1 per million. Incidence rate was age-dependent and rose sharply with age. The overall case fatality rate was 10% (5). The overall weekly excess mortality from agranulocytosis ranged from 0.019 per million for aspirin users to 0.11 per million for dipyrone users. For dipyrone users below 60 years the overall weekly mortality rate was 0.054 per million, and for those over 60 years 0.32 per million. See Tables 1, 2 and 3.

Aplastic anaemia

Aplastic anaemia refers to a diverse group of potentially severe bone-marrow disorders characterized by pancytopenia and a marrow largely devoid of haematopoietic cells. Its clinical features, such as bleeding manifestations, infections, fatigue and pallor, are the effects of too few functional peripheral blood cells. Its annual incidence rate associated with hospital admission is 2.0 per million (5). The fatality rate increases with age; the overall rate is 46% within two years (5). Marrow transplantation has dramatically improved survival, however. The overall weekly excess mortality from aplastic anaemia was 0.063 per million for diclofenac users: 0.04 and 0.18 for under and over 60 years of age, respectively. The rate for the other drugs was not significantly increased above background.

Serious upper gastrointestinal complications

The mechanisms by which NSAIDs cause gastrointestinal injury are those dependent on cyclooxygenase (COX-1) inhibition and those that exert direct toxic effects on the local mucosa. A major protective mechanism against mucosal injury is the concentration of prostaglandin in the gastrointestinal mucosa; it is suppressed by inhibition of cyclooxygenase, the rate-limiting enzyme in the synthesis of prostaglandin. Aspirin inhibits it irreversibly, and most other NSAIDs reversibly.

The reported weekly estimates of incidence rate ranged from 3 to 40 per million. The case fatality rates associated with gastrointestinal complications were 0.023 to 0.098 per million per week and were highest in older age groups (9, 13, 14, 17, 18). In subjects under 60 the weekly rate was 4.6 per million, with a 2.6 per cent case fatality rate. For patients over 60 it was substantially higher (33.8 per million; 9.5 per cent case fatality rate). The rate for the over-60 groups ranged from 2.5 per million per week for ibuprofen users to 9.5 for aspirin users.

Global excess mortality risk

The global excess mortality risk per million short-term drug users per week for all ages was 1.7 for aspirin ≤1000 mg per day, 1.5 for diclofenac ≤100 mg per day, 0.4 for ibuprofen ≤1500 mg per day, 0.05 for paracetamol ≤1500 mg per day and 0.11 for dipyrone ≤1500 mg per day (see Table 1 and Figure 1). The excess mortality associated with gastrointestinal complications had the most important influence on the overall global excess mortality in users of all NSAIDs (aspirin, diclofenac and ibuprofen). Gastrointestinal complications did not contribute to the global excess mortality attributed to paracetamol and dipyrone.

The global excess risk associated with NSAID use in the age group over 60 was an order of magnitude greater than in the under 60 group (Figures 1, 2). Although there was an age-dependent increase in the global excess risk associated with dipyrone use of about fivefold, this excess risk was significantly smaller than the respective risk estimates for aspirin and diclofenac. Paracetamol was significantly associated with SJS/TEN but age-specific estimates were not available.

C. Discussion

The global risk of mortality associated with dipyrone appears to be substantially lower than that associated with equivalent doses of NSAIDs for short-term relief of mild and moderate pain, particularly in the older age group. The estimated weekly excess mortality from agranulocytosis, aplastic anaemia, anaphylaxis and serious upper gastrointestinal complications per million short-term users was 1.7 per million for aspirin, 1.5 per million for diclofenac, 0.4 per million for ibuprofen, 0.05 per million for paracetamol and 0.11 per million for dipyrone.

The overall excess mortality after short-term NSAID use was largely influenced by the excess mortality associated with upper gastrointestinal complications. In the selected doses, the investigated NSAIDs have antipyretic and anti-inflammatory as well as analgesic properties. As the identified epidemiological studies do not provide information on the indication for drug use, it is reasonable to expect that the indication for NSAID use also included inflammatory diseases. The current benefit-risk analysis can thus be considered valid because the risk of potentially life-threatening events is normally not associated with the indication for drug use.

A limitation of this evaluation was the use of relative estimates that did not account for the duration of therapy or for previous therapy with the analgesics under study. It is known, e.g., that the risk of gastrointestinal haemorrhage is higher early during nonsteroidal anti-inflammatory drug use (within one month after initiation), decreasing with duration of treatment. However, for purposes of this evaluation it was assumed that the risk of adverse effects was constant throughout therapy.

Incidence rates and the case-fatality rates of gastrointestinal bleeding and agranulocytosis show a strong age dependency. There were no age-specific data available for the other included adverse events. The global excess risk associated with NSAID use was substantially higher in the age group over 60 years than at younger ages.

D. Conclusion

In order to compare the adverse drug-attributed public health impact of non-narcotic analgesics, an epidemiological perspective was chosen and the drug-related global mortality quantified. The excess mortality associated with gastrointestinal complications exerted the major influence on the overall estimate, contributing to 99% of the excess mortality in NSAID users (aspirin, diclofenac and ibuprofen). In users of paracetamol, the major influence on the global mortality estimate was Stevens-Johnson syndrome and toxic epidermal necrolysis, whereas global mortality attributed to dipyrone was due mainly to agranulocytosis. There was a strong association of the global excess risk with age in NSAID users.

IV. BENEFIT-RISK ASSESSMENT

The benefits of dipyrone are equivalent or superior to those of other non-narcotic analgesics. The relative risk of dipyrone-associated agranulocytosis is substantial but the excess risk is very low. Dipyrone carries a lower risk of fatal complications from potentially fatal adverse events than aspirin or other NSAIDs and the difference is even more pronounced in the over-60 age group.

V. SUMMARY OF ACTION TAKEN

A new methodological approach based on a body of epidemiological studies has shown that the global risk of dipyrone compares favourably with that of competing non-narcotic analgesics and that the risk of agranulocytosis had been overestimated in the evaluation during the 1970s. Although dipyrone no longer has patent protection, Hoechst decided to apply for reapproval in Sweden (where dipyrone is sold as Novalgin).

In 1995, Novalgin 50 mg tablets and Novalgin solution for injection 500 mg/ml were reapproved in Sweden for short-term treatment in acute, moderate to severe pain after tissue injury (e.g., as a result of surgical procedures) and acute, moderate to severe colicky pain (e.g., in the urinary or biliary tract).

VI. POINTS ILLUSTRATED

Drug safety is often evaluated by determining the frequency of occurrence of one particular drug-associated adverse event. This assumes that all other adverse events have an identical profile and frequency. When this is not the case safety can be assessed only by a three-dimensional construct of the qualitative profile of adverse events, their frequency of occurrence, and a common measure of health outcome.

The relative benefit-risk was evaluated from an epidemiological perspective. Death was chosen as the common outcome of the different adverse events, thereby restricting the evaluation to potentially life-threatening events. The drug-related mortality for dipyrone and other non-narcotic analgesics, as a measure of the adverse drug-attributed public-health impact, was estimated and expressed by the excess mortality.

References

(1) DerSimonian N, Laird N: Meta-analysis in clinical trials. *Controlled Clinical Trials* 1987; 7: 177-188.

(2) Buckland ST: Monte Carlo confidence intervals. *Biometrics* 1984; 40: 811-817.

(3) van der Klauw MM, Stricker BHC, Herings RMC, Cost WS, Valkenburg HA, Wilson HP: A population based case-cohort study of drug-induced anaphylaxis. *Brit J Clin Pharmacol* 1993; 35: 400-408

(4) International Collaborative Study of Severe Anaphylaxis. Members of study group: Laporte JR, Latorre FJ, Gadgill DA, Chandrasekhar DV, Laszlo A, Retsagi G, Alfredson L, Martinez C, Kaufman DW, Anderson T, Kelly J, Shapiro S: An epidemiologic study of severe anaphylaxis among hospital patients: methods and incidence. To be published in *Epidemiology* 1998.

(5) Kaufman DW, Kelly JP, Levy M, Shapiro S: The drug etiology of agranulocytosis and aplastic anemia. *Monographs in Epidemiology and Biostatistics*. Volume 18, Oxford University Press 1991.

(6) Roujeau JC, Kelly JP, Naldi L, Rzany B, Stern RS, Anderson T, Auquier A, Bastuji-Garin S, Correia O, Locati F, Mockenhaupt M, Paoletti C, Shapiro S, Sheir N, Schöpf E, Kaufman D: Drug etiology of Stevens-Johnson syndrome and toxic epidermal necrolysis, first results from an international case-control study. *N Engl J Med* 1995; 333: 1600-1609.

(7) Mockenhaupt M, Schlingmann J, Schroeder W, Schoepf E: Evaluation of non-steroidal antiinflammatory drugs (NSAIDs) and muscle relaxants as risk factors for Stevens-Johnson syndrome (SJS) and toxic epidermal necrolysis (TEN). *Pharmacoepidemiology and Drug Safety* 1996; 5:S116.

(8) Schöpf E, Rzany B, Mockenhaupt M: Schwere arzneimittelinduzierte Hautreaktionen: Pemphigus vulgaris, bullöses Pemphigoid, generalized bullous fixed drug eruption, Erythema exsudativum multiforme majus, Stevens-

Johnson-Syndrom und toxisch-epidermale Nekrolyse. *Fortschritte der praktischen Dermatologie und Venerologie* 1994; 89 — 95

(9) Laporte JR, Carné X, Vidal X, Moreno V, Juan J: Upper gastrointestinal bleeding in relation to previous use of analgesics and non-steroidal anti-inflammatory drugs. *Lancet* 1991, 337: 85-89.

(10) Henry D, Robertson J: Nonsteroidal anti-inflammatory drugs and peptic ulcer hospitalization rates in New South Wales. *Gastroenterology* 1993; 104: 1083-1091.

(11) Carson JL, Strom BL, Soper KA, West SL, Morse ML: The association of nonsteroidal anti-inflammatory drugs with upper gastrointestinal tract bleeding. *Arch Intern Med* 1987; 147: 85-88.

(12) Beard K, Walker AM, Perera DR, Jick H: Nonsteroidal anti-inflammatory drugs and hospitalizatiom in gastroesophagal bleeding in the elderly. *Arch Intern Med* 1987, 147: 1621 -1623

(13) Rockall TA, Logan RFA, HB Devlin, Northfield TC on behalf of the steering committee and the members of the national audit of acute upper gastrointestinal haemorrhage. Incidence of and mortality from acute upper gastrointestinal adverse event haemorrhage in the United Kingdom. *BMJ* 1995; 311: 222-230.

(14) Perez Gutthann S, Garcia Rodriguez LA, Raiford DS: Individual nonsteroidal antiinflammatory drugs and other risk factors for upper gastrointestinal bleeding and perforation. *Epidemiology* 1997; 8: 20-24.

(15) Kaufman DW, Kelly JP, Sheehan JE, et al.: Nonsteroidal anti-inflammatory drug use in relation to major upper gastrointestinal bleeding. *Clin Pharmacol Ther* 1993; 53(4): 485-494.

(16) Garcia Rodriguez LA, Jick H: Risk of upper gastrointestinal bleeding and perforation associated with individual non-steroidal anti-inflammatory drugs. *Lancet* 1994; 343: 769-772.

(17) Katschinski BD, Logan RFA, Davies J, Langman MJS: Audit of mortality in upper gastrointestinal bleeding. *Postgrad Med J* 1989; 65: 913-917.

(18) Wilcox CM, Clark WS: Association of nonsteroidal antiinflammatory drugs with outcome in upper and lower gastrointestinal bleeding. *Dig Dis Sci* 1997; 42: 985-989

(19) Carson JL, Strom BL, Duff A, Gupta A, Das K: Safety of nonsteroidal anti-inflammatory drugs with respect to acute liver disease. *Arch Intern Med* 1993; 153: 1331-1336.

(20) Garcia Rodriguez LA, Perez Gutthann S, Walker AM, Lueck L: The role of non-steroidal anti-inflammatory drugs in acute liver injury. *BMJ* 1992; 305: 865-868.

Table 1: Global excess risk of non-narcotic analgesics per million short-term users per week

	Agranulocytosis	Aplastic anaemia	Anaphylaxis	SJS/TEN	GI-bleeding	Global excess risk
incidence rate *case-fatality rate**	0.065 10 %	0.038 45.7 %	0.17 1.6 %	0.035 17.1 %	8.8 6.3 %	
dipyrone	0.10 (0.033–0.23)	ns	0.007 (0.00–0.022)	ns	ns	0.11 (0.04–0.24)
paracetamol	ns	ns	Ns	0.051 (0.016-0.12)		0.05 (0.02–0.12)
NSAIDs						
aspirin	0.019 (0.006–0.042)	ns	0.007 (0.00–0.022)	ns	1.63 (0.70–3.02)	1.66 (0.73-3.04)
diclofenac	ns	0.063 (0.01–0.17)	0.016 (0.00–0.05)	ns	1.42 (0.66–2.50)	1.50 (0.74–2.58)
ibuprofen	ns	ns	Missing data	ns	0.43 (0.00–1.06)	0.43 (0.00–1.06)

ns: relative risk estimate not significant.

* The case fatality rate is the proportion of fatal cases among those who develop an illness.

Table 2: Global excess risk of non-narcotic analgesics per million short-term users per week (age group below 60 years)

	Agranulocytosis	Aplastic anaemia	Anaphylaxis	SJS/TEN	GI-bleeding	Global excess risk
incidence rate *case-fatality rate**	0.040 6.5 %	0.029 39.1 %	0.17 1.6 %	0.035 17.1 %	4.6 2.6 %	
dipyrone	0.054 (0.01–0.17)	ns	0.007 (0.00–0.022)	ns	ns	0.06 (0.01–0.18)
paracetamol	ns	ns	ns	0.051 (0.016-0.12)		0.05 (0.02–0.12)
NSAIDs						
aspirin	ns	ns	0.007 (0.00–0.022)	ns	0.35 (0.11–0.74)	0.38 (0.14–0.77)
diclofenac	ns	0.04 (0.01–0.11)	0.016 (0.00–0.05)	ns	0.31 (0.10–0.62)	0.36 (0.15–0.68)
ibuprofen	ns	ns	Missing data	ns	0.09 (0.00–0.25)	0.09 (0.00–0.25)

ns: relative risk estimate not significant.

* The case fatality rate is the proportion of fatal cases among those who develop an illness.

Table 3: Global excess risk of non-narcotic analgesics per million short-term users per week (age group above 60 years)

	Agranulocytosis	Aplastic anaemia	Anaphylaxis	SJS/TEN	GI-bleeding	Global excess risk
incidence rate	0.065	0.087	0.167	0.035	33.8	
*case-fatality rate**	10%	56.3 %	1.6 %	17.1 %	9.5 %	
dipyrone	0.32 (0.04-1.07)	ns	0.007 (0.00-0.022)	ns	ns	0.33 (0.05-1.08)
paracetamol	ns	ns	—	0.051 (0.01-0.12)	—	0.05 (0.02-0.12)
NSAIDs						
aspirin	ns	ns	0.007 (0.00-0.022)	ns	9.48 (4.01-17.8)	9.51 (4.03-17.8)
diclofenac	ns	0.18 (0.028-0.47)	0.016 (0.00-0.05)	ns	8.27 (3.79-14.7)	8.46 (3.97-14.9)
ibuprofen	ns	ns	Missing data	ns	2.48 (0.02-6.20)	2.48 (0.02-6.20)

ns: relative risk estimate not significant.

*The case fatality rate is the proportion of fatal cases among those who develop an illness

Figure 1. Age above 60 : global excess risk of non-narcotic analgesics

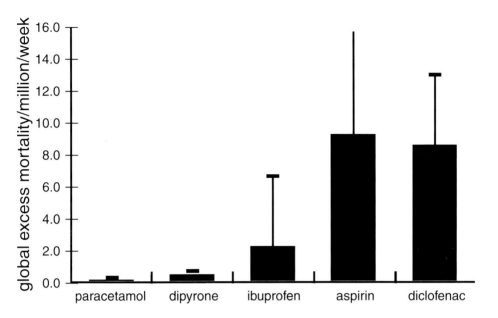

Figure 2. Age below 60 : global excess risk of non-narcotic analgesics

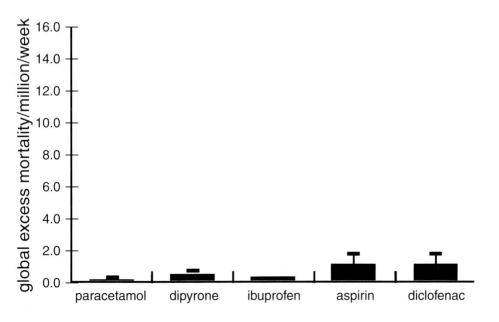

APPENDIX E

THE "TURBO"MODEL
FOR BENEFIT-RISK ANALYSIS

The benefit-risk balance spectrum is portrayed in Figure 1 of Chapter II D. The challenge is to quantify appropriately the benefits and risks so that the drugs under comparison can be represented in their rightful positions on the graph. As already described, both risks and benefits have two basic determinants, degree and probability, which are quantifiable. In its simplest form:

R-factor $= R_o + R_c$

B-factor $= B_o + B_c$

where R_o is the risk associated with the medically most serious adverse effect, R_c represents an additional risk (e.g., the next most serious adverse reaction or the most frequent), $B_o = $ primary benefit, and $B_c = $ ancillary benefits(s). As formulated by Amery, scores for B_o and R_o range from 1 to 5, and for R_c and B_c from 0 to 2. Figure 1 represents an R-score grid with possible scores; measurements should reflect the risk in its most severe appearance (e.g., Torsade de pointe, not QTc prolongation; hepatitis, not transaminase increase), as determined from the best available data (clinical trials, epidemiological data, etc.). Figure 2 presents suggested scores and associated definitions for risk severity. Figure 3 illustrates how to apply them to yield a value for R_c. A similar approach can be used to determine the B-factor (see Figures 4-6). Placement of the resultant B-factor and R-factor on the Turbo diagram (Figure 7) provides a composite for between-drug comparisons.

---

[1] Courtesy of Dr Willem Amery (Jannsen research Foundation, Turnhoutsweg 30, B-2340 Beerse, Belgium)

Figure 1. «R» score associated with the more severe adverse effect (= R)

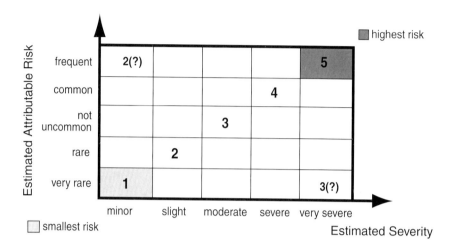

Figure 2. Estimating severity of risk

severity = impact on health status and socioprofessional capabilities

E.g., five scores (definitions are tentative):

1 = some hindrance, but not really incapacitating

2 = temporarily/intermittently incapacitating

3 = incapacitating, but not life-threatening/-shortening

4 = life-shortening, but not life-threatening

5 = life-threatening

Score should refer to risk if properly managed. For example:

preventability through monitoring
(bleeding due to anticoagulant)

(full) recovery if appropriately managed
(hepatotoxicity in most instances)

timely detection (presence of warning signs)

Figure 3. The adjusted "R"score = the "R"-factor

Take the next severe adverse effect or, if there is no other severe adverse effect, the most frequent one and estimate "R"score for this adverse effect = R'

"R"-factor = R_o + correction factor R_c

Correction factor R_c

$= +2$ if R' = 5
$+1$ if R' = 4
$+0$ if R' $\leq$ 3 (tentative example)

Figure 4. «B» score associated with the benefit in that indication (=B_o)

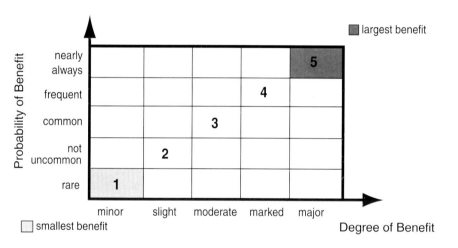

Figure 5. Estimating degree of benefit (B_o)

Benefit = impact on indication as reflected by change(s) in health status and socioprofessional capabilities

E.g., five scores; treated condition becomes (definitions are tentative):

1 = less hindering, but capabilities remain unchanged
2 = less frequently incapacitating or incapability lasts shorter
3 = less incapacitating, but no change in life expectancy
4 = less life-shortening
5 = less immediately life-threatening

Score refers to benefit associated with correctly used medicine (and leaves out of consideration aspects such as non-compliance).

Figure 6. The adjusted "B" score = the "B"-factor

Consider whether the medicine has relevant ancillary properties and assign a value to the correction factor as indicated below:

"B"-factor $= B_o +$ correction factor (B_c) for ancillary property

Correction factor B_c (tentative example)

$= + 2$ if ancillary *medical* property relevant to the indication (e.g., cholesterol lowering effect for antidiabetic or for antihypertensive medicine)

$= + 1$ if ancillary *practical* property (e.g., once-daily dosage schedule or fast onset of action, etc.)

Figure 7. The intrinsic RB balance: the TURBO diagram

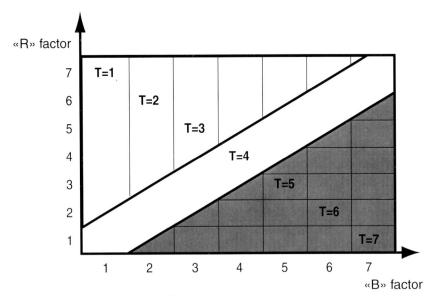

T-scores (in grid) to be further defined

154

APPENDIX F

A SURVEY OF MANUFACTURER AND REGULATORY AUTHORITY DECISION-MAKING PRACTICES FOR POST-MARKETING SAFETY ISSUES

To understand some of the current decision-making practices of companies and regulatory bodies, separate survey questionnaires for each group were designed and distributed to members of the Working Group during the second half of 1995. One company not represented in the Group also completed the survey. The responding parties were as follows:

Manufacturers (11): Burroughs-Wellcome
Ciba-Geigy
Eli Lilly
Genentech
Glaxo
Hoechst
Merck
Pfizer
Roussel Uclaf
Synthélabo
Takeda

(Note: The survey was completed before the Glaxo-Wellcome merger]

Regulators (9): Canada
Denmark
France
Germany
Italy
Japan
Sweden
United Kingdom
United States

The questions and tally of replies are presented below.

Results of survey of manufacturers

1. For major post-marketing safety issues, does your company retain at least one standing committee/established board of outside experts?

Yes – 3   No – 8

If yes, describe its membership, function and frequency of meetings.

> Medical experts,   Monthly – 1
>
> Pharmacoepidemiologists   Quarterly – 2
>
>   No reply – 8

2. If there is no "board" do you *routinely* use individual outside/independent experts for major safety issues?

> Yes – 3   No – 6   No reply – 2

Note: Replies to most of the items of question 3 are summarized in the attached two tables (tables 1 and 2).

3. Please consider a recent significant safety issue/crisis/possible-withdrawal in your company.

    i)   With which drug did it occur?

    ii)   What was the issue?

    iii)   Were outside experts involved   Yes ○   No ○

    iv)   If yes, how were they involved?

    v)   Was an official report developed by the board?   Yes ○   No ○

    vi)   If yes, was it submitted to at least one agency?   Yes ○   No ○

    vii)   Were the criteria used by the board for
    balancing the benefit/risk explicit?   Yes ○   No ○

    viii) If yes, can you provide them?   Yes ○   No ○

(No useful replies to 3 viii)

    ix)   When the agency reviewed the situation:

    [If multiple countries/agencies were involved, describe one major country's effort]

>   *(a)*   was the manufacturer:
>
>   – consulted?   Yes ○   No ○
>
>   – invited to meetings for hearing/testimony?   Yes ○   No ○
>
>   – excluded?   Yes ○   No ○
>
>   *(b)*   Were outside experts involved?   Yes ○   No ○
>
>   *(c)*   If yes, was the debate or opinion made public? Yes ○   No ○
>
>   Which country have you described?

    x)   If the decision was adverse,
    was there an appeal?   Yes ○   No ○

    xi) If yes, how was it done?

156

Results of survey of regulators

1. For major post-marketing safety issues, is your agency served by at least one designated/standing expert committee or board?

Yes – 9   No – 0

2. If yes, is/are board(s) legally mandated?

Yes – 7   No – 2

(Citation for mandate provided for all 7)

3. Please provide details of the board or expert group.

   i)   Number of members: Varied from 5 (2 regulators) to as many as 35

   ii)   Affiliation/Qualifications
         Medicine (1), multidisciplinary (7), specialists (7), consumer (1)

   iii) Frequency of meetings:
         Twice weekly (1), approximately monthly (4), bimonthly (1), quarterly (3)

   iv)   Duration of typical meeting:
         From 2 to 6 hours (4), one day (3), 1-3 days (2)

   v)   Purpose of meeting:
         Exchange of information (3), PMS drug suspension/withdrawal (7), Drug approval/withdrawal (3). Signal identification/confirmation, regulatory action, data analysis, evaluation of ADR reports.

   vi)   Are the recommendations of the board/expert group advisory or binding?

         Advisory (9), Binding (0)

4. If there is no board, do you use individual outside/independent experts for major safety issues?

   Not applicable. Three indicated use of additional experts ad hoc.

   i)   If yes, please give details.
         Traditional remedies (1)

   ii)   What is the mechanism for communication between the expert(s) and regulators? Answer: Ad hoc individuals and groups, telephone, reports.

5. Please consider the most recent major safety issue/crisis/withdrawal. Was this board/expert group involved? (Including ad hoc)

Yes – 9   No – 0

i)   With which drug did it occur?
Third-generation oral contraceptives (5), anorectic (1), felbamate (1), oxytocin + prostaglandin derivatives (1), not specified (1).

ii) What was the issue?
Thromboembolism (5), restricted use (1), aplastic anaemia (1), death and irreversible cerebral damage in mother or baby (1), not specified (1)

iii) If yes, how?
Review data, advise on action.

iv) Were the board/expert groups' deliberations leading to the final decision made public?

Yes – 5   No – 4

v)   Were the criteria used made public?

Yes – 5   No – 3   No response – 1

vi) Were the criteria transparent?

Yes – 5   No – 2   No response – 2

6. When the agency reviewed the situation, was the manufacturer involved in the hearing?

Yes – 5   No – 4

Whether or not present and involved at a hearing, how was the manufacturer involved?

i)   submission of written report

Yes – 7   No – 0   No response – 2

ii) consulted for hearing/testimony

Yes – 7   No – 0   No response – 2

iii) participated in debate

Yes – 4   No – 2   No response – 3

7. What is the mechanism for appeal against such major adverse safety decisions?
There is a process (8): within the same agency (2); with a higher federal agency (1); at minister's office level (2) (one involving a 5-stage process); through administrative courts (3)

MANUFACTURERS SURVEY: REPLIES TO QUESTION 3 (i) – 3 (vii)

Drug Type	Issue	Outside Experts?	Involvement	Official Report	Submitted	Explicit Criteria
Growth hormone	Intracranial hypertension	3	Reviewed case reports, assessed causality	3	3	No (clinical impression)
Anticonvulsant	Severe skin reactions	3	Reviewed case reports, advised on research strategy	No	NA (CIOMS II)	3 (compared with drugs in same class)
Takeda drug	NS	3	NS	No	NA	No
Anxiolytic	Hepatic	No	NA	No	NA	No
Antipsychotic	Haematological	3	Advised (NS)	No	NA	3 (NS)
Anorectic	Pulmonary hypertension	3	Advised on epidemiological study	3	3	Dealt with risk only
Anti-infective	Suicidal behaviour	3	Analyzed pharmacoepi. data	3	No	NA
NSAID	Withdrawal (HRG)	3	Reviewed internal data, critiqued presentations	No	NA	NA
NSAID	Hepatic	3	Evaluated cases, participated in studies	3	3	No
CNS compound	Cardiovascular effects	3	Reviewed cases	No	NA	No
NSAID	NS	?	?	?	?	?

MANUFACTURERS SURVEY: REPLIES TO QUESTION 3 (ix) – 3 (x)

Manufacturer Consulted?	Invited to Meeting	Excluded	Outside Experts	Public?	Country	Appeal?	Comment
Yes	No Mtg	No	Yes	Yes	USA	No	–
Yes	Yes	No	No	–	USA	–	Favourable
Yes	Yes	No	Yes	Yes	France	No	–
Yes	NA	–	–	–	USA	–	Company withdrew ND
Yes	Yes	No	Yes	No	France & Europe	No	–
Yes	Yes	No	Yes	Yes	USA	NA	–
Yes	No	–	Yes	Yes	USA	No	–
Yes	Yes	No	Yes	No	Ireland	NA	Approval but protracted discussions re labelling

NS = not specified

NA = not applicable